CLOUD COMPUTING

Web-Based Applications That Change
the Way You Work and Collaborate Online

Michael Miller

 800 East 96th Street,
India

D1136140

Cloud Computing: Web-Based Applications That Change the Way You Work and Collaborate Online

ISBN-13: 978-0-7897-3803-5

ISBN-10: 0-7897-3803-1

Library of Congress Cataloging-in-Publication data is on file.

Printed in the United States of America

First Printing: August 2008

Trademarks

All terms mentioned in this book that are known to be trademarks or service marks have been appropriately capitalized. Que Publishing cannot attest to the accuracy of this information. Use of a term in this book should not be regarded as affecting the validity of any trademark or service mark.

Warning and Disclaimer

Every effort has been made to make this book as complete and as accurate as possible, but no warranty or fitness is implied. The information provided is on an "as is" basis. The author and the publisher shall have neither liability nor responsibility to any person or entity with respect to any loss or damages arising from the information contained in this book.

Bulk Sales

Que Publishing offers excellent discounts on this book when ordered in quantity for bulk purchases or special sales. For more information, please contact

U.S. Corporate and Government Sales
1-800-382-3419
corpsales@pearsontechgroup.com

For sales outside of the U.S., please contact

International Sales
international@pearson.com

Associate Publisher
Greg Wiegand

Acquisitions Editor
Rick Kughen

Development Editor
Rick Kughen

Managing Editor
Patrick Kanouse

Project Editor
Seth Kerney

Copy Editor
Keith Cline

Indexer
Tim Wright

Proofreader
Paula Lowell

Technical Editor/Reviewer
Aaron Ricadela

Publishing Coordinator
Cindy Teeters

Book Designer
Anne Jones

Page Layout
Bronkella Publishing LLC

Contents at a Glance

Table of Contents

Part I: Understanding Cloud Computing

About the Author

Michael Miller is a successful and prolific author. He is known for his casual, easy-to-read writing style and his ability to explain a wide variety of complex topics to an everyday audience.

Mr. Miller has written more than 80 nonfiction books over the past two decades, with more than a million copies in print. His books for Que include *Absolute Beginner's Guide to Computer Basics, How Microsoft Windows Vista Works, Making a Living from Your eBay Business, Googlepedia: The Ultimate Google Resource,* and *Is It Safe? Protecting Your Computer, Your Business, and Yourself Online.*

You can email Mr. Miller directly at cloud@molehillgroup.com. His website is located at www.molehillgroup.com.

Dedication

To Sherry. Life is a cloud.

Acknowledgments

Thanks to the usual suspects at Que, including but not limited to Greg Wiegand, Rick Kughen, Seth Kerney, Keith Cline, and technical editor Aaron Ricadela.

We Want to Hear from You!

As the reader of this book, *you* are our most important critic and commentator. We value your opinion and want to know what we're doing right, what we could do better, what areas you'd like to see us publish in, and any other words of wisdom you're willing to pass our way.

As an associate publisher for Que Publishing, I welcome your comments. You can email or write me directly to let me know what you did or didn't like about this book—as well as what we can do to make our books better.

Please note that I cannot help you with technical problems related to the topic of this book. We do have a User Services group, however, where I will forward specific technical questions related to the book.

When you write, please be sure to include this book's title and author as well as your name, email address, and phone number. I will carefully review your comments and share them with the author and editors who worked on the book.

Email: feedback@quepublishing.com

Mail: Greg Wiegand
        Associate Publisher
        Que Publishing
        800 East 96th Street
        Indianapolis, IN 46240 USA

Reader Services

Visit our website and register this book at informit.com/register for convenient access to any updates, downloads, or errata that might be available for this book.

Introduction

Introduction

Computing as you know it is about to change: Your applications and documents are going to move from the desktop into the cloud.

I'm talking about cloud computing, where applications and files are hosted on a "cloud" consisting of thousands of computers and servers, all linked together and accessible via the Internet. With cloud computing, everything you do is now web based instead of being desktop based. You can access all your programs and documents from any computer that's connected to the Internet.

How will cloud computing change the way you work? For one thing, you're no longer tied to a single computer. You can take your work anywhere because it's always accessible via the web. In addition, cloud computing facilitates group collaboration, as all group members can access the same programs and documents from wherever they happen to be located.

Cloud computing might sound far-fetched, but chances are you're already using some cloud applications. If you're using a web-based email program, such as Gmail or Hotmail, you're computing in the cloud. If you're using a web-based application such as Google Calendar or Apple MobileMe, you're computing in the cloud. If you're using a file- or photo-sharing site, such as Flickr or Picasa Web Albums, you're computing in the cloud. It's the technology of the future, available to use today.

How does cloud computing work? What does cloud computing mean for the way you use a computer? What are the top cloud computing applications? Good questions all, and all answered in this book: *Cloud Computing: Web-Based Applications That Change the Way You Work and Collaborate Online*. I don't pretend to answer every question you may have (the overly technical ones in particular), but I do try to give you a good solid overview of the cloud computing phenomenon, and introduce you to some of the more popular cloud applications—in particular, those that facilitate group collaboration.

And that's where cloud computing really shines. Whether you want to share photographs with family members, coordinate volunteers for a community organization, or manage a multifaceted project in a large organization, cloud computing can help you collaborate and communicate with other group members. You'll have a better idea of how this works after you read the book, but trust me on this one—if you need to collaborate, cloud computing is the way to do it.

How This Book Is Organized

Cloud computing is actually a pretty simple concept, but one with lots of variations and ramifications. To help you better understand what cloud computing is and what it does, I've organized this book into four major parts:

- Part I, "Understanding Cloud Computing," is the place for you to start learning about cloud computing. I explain how cloud computing works and examine which types of users can best benefit from this new technology.

- Part II, "Cloud Computing for Everyone," examines the practical benefit of cloud computing for users in three different scenarios: in the family, in the community, and in the large organization.

- Part III, "Using Cloud Services," is an overview of various types of web-based applications. You'll learn about cloud services for scheduling, contact management, project management, word processing, presentations, and other key applications.

- Part IV, "Outside the Cloud: Other Ways to Collaborate Online," moves beyond strict cloud computing to examine other Internet-based tools for group collaboration, including web email, instant messaging, social networks, online groupware, blogs, and wikis.

Taken together, the 20 chapters in this book provide an excellent overview of cloud computing. If you're not sure what cloud computing is yet, you will be when you get done reading this book.

Conventions Used in This Book

I hope that this book is easy enough to figure out on its own, without requiring its own instruction manual. As you read through the pages, however, it helps to know precisely how I've presented specific types of information.

Web Page Addresses

There are a lot of web page addresses in this book. They're noted as such:

www.molehillgroup.com

Technically, a web page address is supposed to start with http:// (as in http://www.molehillgroup.com). Because Internet Explorer and other web browsers automatically insert this piece of the address, however, you don't have to type it—and I haven't included it in any of the addresses in this book.

Cloud Services

I also list a lot of web-based applications and services in this book; after all, that's what cloud computing is all about. Know, however, that companies are constantly changing prices, coming out with new features, introducing completely new services, and discontinuing older ones. With that in mind, every service and URL listed in this book is valid as of June 2008; chances are, however, that something will change by the time you read the book.

Special Elements

This book includes two special elements that provide additional information not included in the basic text. These elements are designed to supplement the text to make it your learning faster, easier, and more efficient.

In addition, I end each chapter with a sidebar—a chunk of text that goes beyond what is presented in the normal chapter text to provide additional information that may be of interest to you. I find these sidebars interesting but not necessarily essential; you may or may not feel the same.

note A note is designed to provide information that is generally useful but not specifically necessary for what you're doing at the moment.

Let Me Know What You Think

tip A tip offers additional advice that might prove useful to the task at hand.

I always love to hear from readers. If you want to contact me, feel free to email me at cloud@molehillgroup.com. I can't promise that I'll answer every message, but I do promise to read each one!

caution A caution warns you of a particular situation—be alert to the warning!

If you want to learn more about me and any new books I have cooking, check out my Molehill Group website at www.molehillgroup.com. Who knows—you might find some other books there that you'd like to read.

PART

I

Understanding Cloud Computing

1

Beyond the Desktop: An Introduction to Cloud Computing

I n a world that sees new technological trends bloom and fade on almost a daily basis, one new trend promises more longevity. This trend is called *cloud computing*, and it will change the way you use your computer and the Internet.

Cloud computing portends a major change in how we store information and run applications. Instead of running programs and data on an individual desktop computer, everything is hosted in the "cloud"—a nebulous assemblage of computers and servers accessed via the Internet. Cloud computing lets you access all your applications and documents from anywhere in the world, freeing you from the confines of the desktop and making it easier for group members in different locations to collaborate.

The emergence of cloud computing is the computing equivalent of the electricity revolution of a century ago. Before the advent of electrical utilities, every farm and business produced its own electricity from freestanding generators. After the electrical grid was created, farms and businesses shut down their generators and bought electricity from the utilities, at a much lower price (and with much greater reliability) than they could produce on their own.

Look for the same type of revolution to occur as cloud computing takes hold. The desktop-centric notion of computing that we hold today is bound to fall by the wayside as we come to expect the universal access, 24/7 reliability, and ubiquitous collaboration promised by cloud computing.

It is the way of the future.

Cloud Computing: What It Is—and What It Isn't

With traditional desktop computing, you run copies of software programs on each computer you own. The documents you create are stored on the computer on which they were created. Although documents can be accessed from other computers on the network, they can't be accessed by computers outside the network.

The whole scene is PC-centric.

With cloud computing, the software programs you use aren't run from your personal computer, but are rather stored on servers accessed via the Internet. If your computer crashes, the software is still available for others to use. Same goes for the documents you create; they're stored on a collection of servers accessed via the Internet. Anyone with permission can not only access the documents, but can also edit and collaborate on those documents in real time. Unlike traditional computing, this cloud computing model isn't PC-centric, it's document-centric. Which PC you use to access a document simply isn't important.

But that's a simplification. Let's look in more detail at what cloud computing is—and, just as important, what it isn't.

What Cloud Computing Isn't

First, cloud computing isn't network computing. With network computing, applications/documents are hosted on a single company's server and accessed over the company's network. Cloud computing is a lot bigger than that. It encompasses multiple companies, multiple servers, and multiple networks. Plus, unlike network computing, cloud services and storage are accessible from anywhere in the world over an Internet connection; with network computing, access is over the company's network only.

Cloud computing also isn't traditional outsourcing, where a company farms out (subcontracts) its computing services to an outside firm. While an outsourcing firm might host a company's data or applications, those documents and programs are only accessible to the company's employees via the company's network, not to the entire world via the Internet.

So, despite superficial similarities, networking computing and outsourcing are not cloud computing.

What Cloud Computing Is

Key to the definition of cloud computing is the "cloud" itself. For our purposes, the cloud is a large group of interconnected computers. These computers can be personal computers or network servers; they can be public or private.

For example, Google hosts a cloud that consists of both smallish PCs and larger servers. Google's cloud is a private one (that is, Google owns it) that is publicly accessible (by Google's users).

This cloud of computers extends beyond a single company or enterprise. The applications and data served by the cloud are available to broad group of users, cross-enterprise and cross-platform. Access is via the Internet. Any authorized user can access these docs and apps from any computer over any Internet connection. And, to the user, the technology and infrastructure behind the cloud is invisible. It isn't apparent (and, in most cases doesn't matter) whether cloud services are based on HTTP, HTML, XML, JavaScript, or other specific technologies.

It might help to examine how one of the pioneers of cloud computing, Google, perceives the topic. From Google's perspective, there are six key properties of cloud computing:

- Cloud computing is user-centric. Once you as a user are connected to the cloud, whatever is stored there—documents, messages, images, applications, whatever—becomes yours. In addition, not only is the data yours, but you can also share it with others. In effect, any device that accesses your data in the cloud also becomes yours.

- Cloud computing is task-centric. Instead of focusing on the application and what it can do, the focus is on what you need done and how the application can do it for you., Traditional applications—word processing, spreadsheets, email, and so on—are becoming less important than the documents they create.

- Cloud computing is powerful. Connecting hundreds or thousands of computers together in a cloud creates a wealth of computing power impossible with a single desktop PC.

- Cloud computing is accessible. Because data is stored in the cloud, users can instantly retrieve more information from multiple repositories. You're not limited to a single source of data, as you are with a desktop PC.

- Cloud computing is intelligent. With all the various data stored on the computers in a cloud, data mining and analysis are necessary to access that information in an intelligent manner.

- Cloud computing is programmable. Many of the tasks necessary with cloud computing must be automated. For example, to protect the integrity of the data, information stored on a single computer in the cloud must be replicated on other computers in the cloud. If that one computer goes offline, the cloud's programming automatically redistributes that computer's data to a new computer in the cloud.

All these definitions behind us, what constitutes cloud computing in the real world?

As you'll learn throughout this book, a raft of web-hosted, Internet-accessible, group-collaborative applications are currently available, with many more on the way. Perhaps the best and most popular examples of cloud computing applications today are the Google family of applications—Google Docs & Spreadsheets, Google Calendar, Gmail, Picasa, and the like. All of these applications are hosted on Google's servers, are accessible to any user with an Internet connection, and can be used for group collaboration from anywhere in the world.

In short, cloud computing enables a shift from the computer to the user, from applications to tasks, and from isolated data to data that can be accessed from anywhere and shared with anyone. The user no longer has to take on the task of data management; he doesn't even have to remember where the data is. All that matters is that the data is in the cloud, and thus immediately available to that user and to other authorized users.

note Developers and IT types might have a slightly different definition of cloud computing than that for an end user. To the people who develop and manage computer systems, cloud computing is all about horizontal scalability in the form of server capability; the technical challenge is developing operating systems and applications to manage this sort of on-the-fly scaling—while keeping the mechanics of it invisible to the end user.

From Collaboration to the Cloud: A Short History of Cloud Computing

Cloud computing has as its antecedents both client/server computing and peer-to-peer distributed computing. It's all a matter of how centralized storage facilitates collaboration and how multiple computers work together to increase computing power.

Client/Server Computing: Centralized Applications and Storage

In the antediluvian days of computing (pre-1980 or so), everything operated on the *client/server* model. All the software applications, all the data, and all the control resided on huge mainframe computers, otherwise known as *servers*. If a user wanted to access specific data or run a program, he had to connect to the mainframe, gain appropriate access, and then do his business while essentially "renting" the program or data from the server.

Users connected to the server via a computer terminal, sometimes called a workstation or *client*. This computer was sometimes called a *dumb terminal* because it didn't have a lot (if any!) memory, storage space, or processing power. It was merely a device that connected the user to and enabled him to use the mainframe computer.

Users accessed the mainframe only when granted permission, and the information technology (IT) staff weren't in the habit of handing out access casually. Even on a mainframe computer, processing power is limited—and the IT staff were the guardians of that power. Access was not immediate, nor could two users access the same data at the same time.

Beyond that, users pretty much had to take whatever the IT staff gave them—with no variations. Want to customize a report to show only a subset of the normal information? Can't do it. Want to create a new report to look at some new data? You can't do it, although the IT staff can—but on their schedule, which might be weeks from now.

The fact is, when multiple people are sharing a single computer, even if that computer is a huge mainframe, you have to wait your turn. Need to rerun a financial report? No problem—if you don't mind waiting until this afternoon, or tomorrow morning. There isn't always immediate access in a client/server environment, and seldom is there immediate gratification.

So the client/server model, while providing similar centralized storage, differed from cloud computing in that it did not have a user-centric focus; with client/server computing, all the control rested with the mainframe—and with the guardians of that single computer. It was not a user-enabling environment.

Peer-to-Peer Computing: Sharing Resources

As you can imagine, accessing a client/server system was kind of a "hurry up and wait" experience. The server part of the system also created a huge bottleneck. All communications between computers had to go through the server first, however inefficient that might be.

The obvious need to connect one computer to another without first hitting the server led to the development of *peer-to-peer* (P2P) computing. P2P computing defines a network architecture in which each computer has equivalent capabilities and responsibilities. This is in contrast to the traditional client/server network architecture, in which one or more computers are dedicated to serving the others. (This relationship is sometimes characterized as a master/slave relationship, with the central server as the master and the client computer as the slave.)

P2P was an equalizing concept. In the P2P environment, every computer is a client *and* a server; there are no masters and slaves. By recognizing all computers on the network as peers, P2P enables direct exchange of resources and services. There is no need for a central server, because any computer can function in that capacity when called on to do so.

P2P was also a decentralizing concept. Control is decentralized, with all computers functioning as equals. Content is also dispersed among the various peer computers. No centralized server is assigned to host the available resources and services.

Perhaps the most notable implementation of P2P computing is the Internet. Many of today's users forget (or never knew) that the Internet was initially conceived, under its original ARPAnet guise, as a peer-to-peer system that would share computing resources across the United States. The various ARPAnet sites—and there weren't many of them—were connected together not as clients and servers, but as equals.

The P2P nature of the early Internet was best exemplified by the Usenet network. Usenet, which was created back in 1979, was a network of computers (accessed via the Internet), each of which hosted the entire contents of the network. Messages were propagated between the peer computers; users connecting to any single Usenet server had access to all (or substantially all) the messages posted to each individual server. Although the users' connection to the Usenet server was of the traditional client/server nature, the relationship between the Usenet servers was definitely P2P—and presaged the cloud computing of today.

That said, not every part of the Internet is P2P in nature. With the development of the World Wide Web came a shift away from P2P back to the client/server model. On the web, each website is served up by a group of computers, and sites' visitors use client software (web browsers) to access it. Almost all content is centralized, all control is centralized, and the clients have no autonomy or control in the process.

Distributed Computing: Providing More Computing Power

One of the most important subsets of the P2P model is that of *distributed computing*, where idle PCs across a network or across the Internet are tapped to provide computing power for large, processor-intensive projects. It's a simple concept, all about *cycle sharing* between multiple computers.

A personal computer, running full-out 24 hours a day, 7 days a week, is capable of tremendous computing power. Most people don't use their computers 24/7, however, so a good portion of a computer's resources go unused. Distributed computing uses those resources.

When a computer is enlisted for a distributed computing project, software is installed on the machine to run various processing activities during those periods when the PC is typically unused. The results of that spare-time processing are periodically uploaded to the distributed computing network, and combined with similar results from other PCs in the project. The result, if enough computers are involved, simulates the processing power of much larger mainframes and supercomputers—which is necessary for some very large and complex computing projects.

For example, genetic research requires vast amounts of computing power. Left to traditional means, it might take years to solve essential mathematical problems. By connecting together thousands (or millions) of individual PCs, more power is applied to the problem, and the results are obtained that much sooner.

Distributed computing dates back to 1973, when multiple computers were networked together at the Xerox PARC labs and worm software was developed to cruise through the network looking for idle resources. A more practical application of distributed computing appeared in 1988, when researchers at the DEC (Digital Equipment Corporation) System Research Center developed software that distributed the work to factor large numbers among workstations within their laboratory. By 1990, a group of about 100 users, utilizing this software, had factored a 100-digit number. By 1995, this same effort had been expanded to the web to factor a 130-digit number.

It wasn't long before distributed computing hit the Internet. The first major Internet-based distributed computing project was distributed.net, launched in 1997, which employed thousands of personal computers to crack encryption codes. Even bigger was SETI@home, launched in May 1999, which linked together millions of individual computers to search for intelligent life in outer space.

Many distributed computing projects are conducted within large enterprises, using traditional network connections to form the distributed computing network. Other, larger, projects utilize the computers of everyday Internet users, with the computing typically taking place offline, and then uploaded once a day via traditional consumer Internet connections.

Collaborative Computing: Working as a Group

From the early days of client/server computing through the evolution of P2P, there has been a desire for multiple users to work simultaneously on the same computer-based project. This type of collaborative computing is the driving force behind cloud computing, but has been around for more than a decade.

Early group collaboration was enabled by the combination of several different P2P technologies. The goal was (and is) to enable multiple users to collaborate on group projects online, in real time.

To collaborate on any project, users must first be able to talk to one another. In today's environment, this means instant messaging for text-based communication, with optional audio/telephony and video capabilities for voice and picture communication. Most collaboration systems offer the complete range of audio/video options, for full-featured multiple-user video conferencing.

In addition, users must be able to share files and have multiple users work on the same document simultaneously. Real-time whiteboarding is also common, especially in corporate and education environments.

Early group collaboration systems ranged from the relatively simple (Lotus Notes and Microsoft NetMeeting) to the extremely complex (the building-block architecture of the Groove Networks system). Most were targeted at large corporations, and limited to operation over the companies' private networks.

note *Whiteboarding* is where one or more users "draw" on a virtual whiteboard that is viewable by all the members of the group.

Cloud Computing: The Next Step in Collaboration

note The term *cloud computing* is a relatively recent one, gaining prominence in 2007 as a means of describing Internet-based distributed computing and its associated applications.

With the growth of the Internet, there was no need to limit group collaboration to a single enterprise's network environment. Users from multiple locations within a corporation, and from multiple organizations, desired to collaborate on projects that crossed company and geographic boundaries. To do this, projects had to be housed in the "cloud" of the Internet, and accessed from any Internet-enabled location.

The concept of cloud-based documents and services took wing with the development of large server farms, such as those run by Google and other search companies. Google already had a collection of servers that it used to power its massive search engine; why not use that same computing power to drive a collection of web-based applications—and, in the process, provide a new level of Internet-based group collaboration?

That's exactly what happened, although Google wasn't the only company offering cloud computing solutions. On the infrastructure side, IBM, Sun Systems, and other big iron providers are offering the hardware necessary to build cloud networks. On the software side, dozens of companies are developing cloud-based applications and storage services.

Today, people are using cloud services and storage to create, share, find, and organize information of all different types. Tomorrow, this functionality will be available not only to computer users, but to users of any device that connects to the Internet—mobile phones, portable music players, even automobiles and home television sets.

The Network Is the Computer: How Cloud Computing Works

Sun Microsystems's slogan is "The network is the computer," and that's as good as any to describe how cloud computing works. In essence, a network of computers functions as a single computer to serve data and applications to users over the Internet. The network exists in the "cloud" of IP addresses that we know as the Internet, offers massive computing power and storage capability, and enables widescale group collaboration.

But that's the simple explanation. Let's take a look at how cloud computing works in more detail.

Understanding Cloud Architecture

The key to cloud computing is the "cloud"—a massive network of servers or even individual PCs interconnected in a grid. These computers run in parallel, combining the resources of each to generate supercomputing-like power.

What, exactly, is the "cloud"? Put simply, the cloud is a collection of computers and servers that are publicly accessible via the Internet. This hardware is typically owned and operated by a third party on a consolidated basis in one or more data center locations. The machines can run any combination of operating systems; it's the processing power of the machines that matter, not what their desktops look like.

As shown in Figure 1.1, individual users connect to the cloud from their own personal computers or portable devices, over the Internet. To these individual users, the cloud is seen as a single application, device, or document. The hardware in the cloud (and the operating system that manages the hardware connections) is invisible.

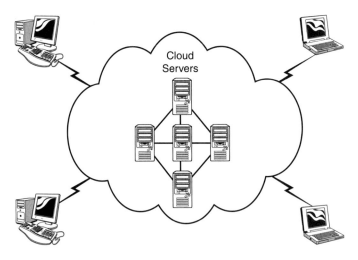

FIGURE 1.1

How users connect to the cloud.

This cloud architecture is deceptively simple, although it does require some intelligent management to connect all those computers together and assign task processing to multitudes of users. As you can see in Figure 1.2, it all starts with the front-end interface seen by individual users. This is how users select a task or service (either starting an application or opening a document). The user's request then gets passed to the system management, which finds the correct resources and then calls the system's appropriate provisioning services. These services carve out the necessary resources in the cloud, launch the appropriate web application, and either creates or opens the requested document. After the web application is launched, the system's monitoring and metering functions track the usage of the cloud so that resources are apportioned and attributed to the proper user(s).

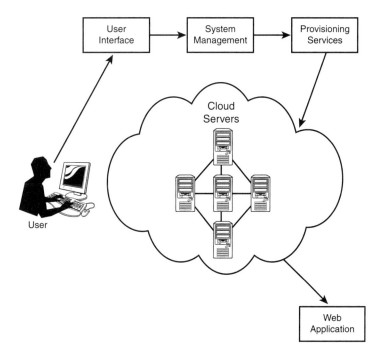

FIGURE 1.2

The architecture behind a cloud computing system.

As you can see, key to the notion of cloud computing is the automation of many management tasks. The system isn't a cloud if it requires human management to allocate processes to resources. What you have in this instance is merely a twenty-first-century version of old-fashioned data center–based client/server computing. For the system to attain cloud status, manual management must be replaced by automated processes.

Understanding Cloud Storage

One of the primary uses of cloud computing is for data storage. With *cloud storage*, data is stored on multiple third-party servers, rather than on the dedicated servers used in traditional networked data storage.

When storing data, the user sees a *virtual server*—that is, it appears as if the data is stored in a particular place with a specific name. But that place doesn't exist in reality. It's just a pseudonym used to reference virtual space carved out of the cloud. In reality, the user's data could be stored on any one or more of the computers used to create the cloud. The actual storage location may even differ from day to day or even minute to minute, as the cloud dynamically manages available storage space. But even though the location is virtual, the user sees a "static" location for his data—and can actually manage his storage space as if it were connected to his own PC.

Cloud storage has both financial and security-associated advantages. Financially, virtual resources in the cloud are typically cheaper than dedicated physical resources connected to a personal computer or network. As for security, data stored in the cloud is secure from accidental erasure or hardware crashes, because it is duplicated across multiple physical machines; since multiple copies of the data are kept continually, the cloud continues to function as normal even if one or more machines go offline. If one machine crashes, the data is duplicated on other machines in the cloud.

Understanding Cloud Services

Any web-based application or service offered via cloud computing is called a *cloud service*. Cloud services can include anything from calendar and contact applications to word processing and presentations. Almost all large computing companies today, from Google to Amazon to Microsoft, are developing various types of cloud services.

With a cloud service, the application itself is hosted in the cloud. An individual user runs the application over the Internet, typically within a web browser. The browser accesses the cloud service and an instance of the application is opened within the browser window. Once launched, the web-based application operates and behaves like a standard desktop application. The only difference is that the application and the working documents remain on the host's cloud servers.

Cloud services offer many advantages. If the user's PC crashes, it doesn't affect either the host application or the open document; both remain unaffected in the cloud. In addition, an individual user can access his applications and documents from any location on any PC. He doesn't have to have a copy of every app and file with him when he moves from office to home to remote location. Finally, because documents are hosted in the cloud, multiple users can collaborate on the same document in real time, using any available Internet connection. Documents are no longer machine-centric. Instead, they're always available to any authorized user.

Companies in the Cloud: Cloud Computing Today

We're currently in the early days of the cloud computing revolution. Although many cloud services are available today, more and more interesting applications are still in development. That said, cloud computing today is attracting the best and biggest companies from across the computing industry, all of whom hope to establish profitable business models based in the cloud.

As discussed earlier in this chapter, perhaps the most noticeable company currently embracing the cloud computing model is Google. As you'll see throughout this book, Google offers a powerful collection of web-based applications, all served via its cloud architecture. Whether you want cloud-based word processing (Google Docs), presentation software (Google Presentations), email (Gmail), or calendar/scheduling functionality (Google Calendar), Google has an offering. And best of all, Google is adept in getting all of its web-based applications to interface with each other; their cloud services are interconnected to the user's benefit.

Other major companies are also involved in the development of cloud services. Microsoft, for example, offers its Windows Live suite of web-based applications, as well as the Live Mesh initiative that promises to link together all types of devices, data, and applications in a common cloud-based platform. Amazon has its Elastic Compute Cloud (EC2), a web service that provides cloud-based resizable computing capacity for application developers. IBM has established a Cloud Computing Center to deliver cloud services and research to clients. And numerous smaller companies have launched their own web-based applications, primarily (but not exclusively) to exploit the collaborative nature of cloud services.

As we work through this book, we'll examine many of these companies and their offerings. All you need to know for now is that there's a big future in cloud computing—and everybody's jumping on the bandwagon.

Why Cloud Computing Matters

Why is cloud computing important? There are many implications of cloud technology, for both developers and end users.

For developers, cloud computing provides increased amounts of storage and processing power to run the applications they develop. Cloud computing also enables new ways to access information, process and analyze data, and connect people and resources from any location anywhere in the world. In essence, it takes the lid off the box; with cloud computing, developers are no longer boxed in by physical constraints.

For end users, cloud computing offers all those benefits and more. A person using a web-based application isn't physically bound to a single PC, location, or network. His applications and documents can be accessed wherever he is, whenever he wants. Gone is the fear of losing data if a computer crashes. Documents hosted in the cloud always exist, no matter what happens to the user's machine. And then there's the benefit of group collaboration. Users from around the world can collaborate on the same documents, applications, and projects, in real time. It's a whole new world of collaborative computing, all enabled by the notion of cloud computing.

And cloud computing does all this at lower costs, because the cloud enables more efficient sharing of resources than does traditional network computing. With cloud computing, hardware doesn't have to be physically adjacent to a firm's office or data center. Cloud infrastructure can be located anywhere, including and especially areas with lower real estate and electricity costs. In addition, IT departments don't have to engineer for peak-load capacity, because the peak load can be spread out among the external assets in the cloud. And, because additional cloud resources are always at the ready, companies no longer have to purchase assets for infrequent intensive computing tasks. If you need more processing power, it's always there in the cloud—and accessible on a cost-efficient basis.

CLOUD COMPUTING AND WEB 2.0: SEPARATED AT BIRTH?

If you're at all familiar with the concept of cloud computing, you've probably also heard of something called Web 2.0—which, on the surface, sounds suspiciously similar to cloud computing. In fact, cloud computing *is* similar to Web 2.0; in many ways, the one is a subset of the other.

What exactly is Web 2.0? To my mind, it's a bit of a buzzword that different people define in different ways. Tim O'Reilly, the so-called Godfather of Web 2.0, defines it as "the network as platform, spanning all connected devices." Others define the concept of Web 2.0 as a transition from isolated information silos (Web 1.0) to interlinked computing platforms that function like locally available software in the perception of the user. Still others define Web 2.0 in collaborative terms, because all the websites get their value from the actions of users.

These definitions of Web 2.0 sound a lot like cloud computing, but without the technological underpinnings. That is, cloud computing is defined by its architecture and infrastructure (a grid of interconnected computers/servers functioning as a whole), whereas Web 2.0 is defined by how the user sees/is serviced by the system. In other words, cloud computing is about computers; Web 2.0 is about people.

Or, as Tim O'Reilly puts it:

> Cloud computing refers specifically to the use of the Internet as a computing platform; Web 2.0, as I've defined it, is an attempt to explore and explain the business rules of that platform.

Perhaps the terms *cloud computing* and *Web 2.0* are just two different ways of looking at the same phenomenon. Or, equally likely, perhaps cloud computing is a specific Web 2.0 technology. In any instance, know that both terms sprang up at about the same point on computing's evolutionary timeline, and both concepts promise similar results to end users.

At the end of the day, it doesn't matter whether you view something like Google Docs or Microsoft Live Mesh as a cloud service or a Web 2.0 application, or as both. What matters more than a particular label is how that technology impacts the user. In this respect, both cloud computing and Web 2.0 offer very real benefits for all involved.

Are You Ready for Computing in the Cloud?

Cloud computing might be the next big thing, but that doesn't make it the best thing for everyone. Knowing what we know about cloud computing and how it works, how do you know whether cloud computing is right for you?

To answer that question, we must first examine the pros and cons of cloud computing, as well as analyze what types of users benefit most from what cloud computing offers. Then, and only then, can you determine whether you want to jump onto the cloud computing bandwagon.

The Pros and Cons of Cloud Computing

Any serious analysis of cloud computing must address the advantages and disadvantages offered by this burgeoning technology. What's good—and what's bad—about cloud computing? Let's take a look.

Cloud Computing: Advantages

We'll start with the advantages offered by cloud computing—and there are many.

Lower-Cost Computers for Users

Here's a quantitative financial advantage: You don't need a high-powered (and accordingly high-priced) computer to run cloud computing's web-based applications. Because the application runs in the cloud, not on the desktop PC, that desktop PC doesn't need the processing power or hard disk space demanded by traditional desktop software. Hence the client computers in cloud computing can be lower priced, with smaller hard disks, less memory, more efficient processors, and the like. In fact, a client computer in this scenario wouldn't even need a CD or DVD drive, because no software programs have to be loaded and no document files need to be saved.

Improved Performance

Let's look further at what results when a desktop PC doesn't have to store and run a ton of software-based applications. (The apps are run from the cloud, instead.) With fewer bloated programs hogging the computer's memory, users will see better performance from their PCs. Put simply, computers in a cloud computing system will boot up faster and run faster, because they'll have fewer programs and processes loaded into memory.

note This concept of a lower-cost cloud computing client mirrors the New Internet Computer (and the company of the same name) championed by Oracle's Larry Ellison way back in 2000. Ellison's NIC was essentially a workstation with just a processor, keyboard, and monitor—no hard drive or CD/DVD drive—that would be connected via the Internet to a central supercomputer that hosted applications in files. Replace the NIC's single supercomputer with a supercomputer-like grid of computers and you have cloud computing today.

Lower IT Infrastructure Costs

In a larger organization, the IT department could also see lower costs from the adoption of the cloud computing paradigm. Instead of investing in larger numbers of more powerful servers, the IT staff can use the computing power of the cloud to supplement or replace internal computing resources. Those companies that have peak needs no longer have to purchase equipment to handle the peaks (and then lay fallow the rest of the time); peak computing needs are easily handled by computers and servers in the cloud.

Fewer Maintenance Issues

Speaking of maintenance costs, cloud computing greatly reduces both hardware and software maintenance for organizations of all sizes.

First, the hardware. With less hardware (fewer servers) necessary in the organization, maintenance costs are immediately lowered. As to software maintenance, remember that all cloud apps are based elsewhere, so there's no software on the organization's computers for the IT staff to maintain. It's that simple.

Lower Software Costs

Then there's the issue of software cost. Instead of purchasing separate software packages for each computer in the organization, only those employees actually using an application need access to that application in the cloud. Even if it costs the same to use web-based applications as it does similar desktop software (which it probably won't), IT staffs are saved the cost of installing and maintaining those programs on every desktop in the organization.

As to the cost of that software, it's possible that some cloud computing companies will charge as much to "rent" their apps as traditional software companies charge for software purchases. However, early indications are that cloud services will be priced substantially lower than similar desktop software. In fact, many companies (such as Google) are offering their web-based applications for free—which to both individuals and large organizations is much more attractive than the high costs charged by Microsoft and similar desktop software suppliers.

Instant Software Updates

Another software-related advantage to cloud computing is that users are no longer faced with the choice between obsolete software and high upgrade costs. When the app is web-based, updates happen automatically and are available the next time the user logs in to the cloud. Whenever you access a web-based application, you're getting the latest version—without needing to pay for or download an upgrade.

Increased Computing Power

This is an obvious one. When you're tied into a cloud computing system, you have the power of the entire cloud at your disposal. You're no longer limited to what a single desktop PC can do, but can now perform supercomputing-like tasks utilizing the power of thousands of computers and servers. In other words, you can attempt greater tasks in the cloud than you can on your desktop.

Unlimited Storage Capacity

Similarly, the cloud offers virtually limitless storage capacity. Consider that when your desktop or laptop PC is running out of storage space. Your computer's 200GB hard drive is peanuts compared to the hundreds of petabytes (a million gigabytes) available in the cloud. Whatever you need to store, you can.

Increased Data Safety

And all that data you store in the cloud? It stays in the cloud—somewhere. Unlike desktop computing, where a hard disk crash can destroy all your valuable data, a computer crashing in the cloud doesn't affect the storage of your data. That's because data in the cloud is automatically duplicated, so nothing is ever lost. That also means if your personal computer crashes, all your data is still out there in the cloud, still accessible. In a world where few individual desktop PC users back up their data on a regular basis, cloud computing can keep data safe.

Improved Compatibility Between Operating Systems

Ever try to get a Windows-based computer to talk to a Mac? Or a Linux machine to share data with a Windows PC? It can be frustrating.

Not so with cloud computing. In the cloud, operating systems simply don't matter. You can connect your Windows computer to the cloud and share documents with computers running Apple's Mac OS, Linux, or UNIX. In the cloud, the data matters, not the operating system.

Improved Document Format Compatibility

You also don't have to worry about the documents you create on your machine being compatible with other users' applications or operating systems. In a world where Word 2007 documents can't be opened on a computer running Word 2003, all documents created by web-based applications can be read by any other user accessing that application. There are no format incompatibilities when everyone is sharing docs and apps in the cloud.

Easier Group Collaboration

Sharing documents leads directly to collaborating on documents. To many users, this is one of the most important advantages of cloud computing—the ability for multiple users to easily collaborate on documents and projects.

Imagine that you, a colleague in your West Coast office, and a consultant in Europe all need to work together on an important project. Before cloud computing, you had to email or snail mail the relevant documents from one user to another, and work on them sequentially. Not so with cloud computing. Now each of you can access the project's documents simultaneously; the edits one user makes are automatically reflected in what the other users see onscreen. It's all possible, of course, because the documents are hosted in the cloud, not on any of your individual computers. All you need is a computer with an Internet connection, and you're collaborating.

Of course, easier group collaboration means faster completion of most group projects, with full participation from all involved. It also enables group projects across different geographic locations. No longer does the group have to reside in a single office for best effect. With cloud computing, anyone anywhere can collaborate in real time. It's an enabling technology.

Universal Access to Documents

Ever get home from work and realize you left an important document at the office? Or forget to take a file with you on the road? Or get to a conference and discover you forgot to bring along your presentation?

Not a problem—not anymore, anyway. With cloud computing, you don't take your documents with you. Instead, they stay in the cloud, where you can access them from anywhere you have a computer and an Internet connection. All your documents are instantly available from wherever you are. There's simply no need to take your documents with you—as long as you have an Internet connection, that is.

Latest Version Availability

And here's another document-related advantage of cloud computing. When you edit a document at home, that edited version is what you see when you access the document at work. The cloud always hosts the latest version of your documents; you're never in danger of having an outdated version on the computer you're working on.

Removes the Tether to Specific Devices

Finally, here's the ultimate cloud computing advantage—you're no longer tethered to a single computer or network. Change computers, and your existing applications and documents follow you through the cloud. Move to a portable device, and your apps and docs are still available. There's no need to buy a special version of a program for a particular device, or save your document in a device-specific format. Your documents and the programs that created them are the same no matter what computer you're using.

Cloud Computing: Disadvantages

That's not to say, of course, that cloud computing is without its disadvantages. There are a number of reasons why you might not want to adopt cloud computing for your particular needs. Let's examine a few of the risks related to cloud computing.

Requires a Constant Internet Connection

Cloud computing is, quite simply, impossible if you can't connect to the Internet. Because you use the Internet to connect to both your applications and documents, if you don't have an Internet connection, you can't access anything, even your own documents. A dead Internet connection means no work, period—and in areas where Internet connections are few or inherently unreliable, this could be a deal breaker. When you're offline, cloud computing just doesn't work.

This might be a more significant disadvantage than you might think. Sure, you're used to a relatively consistent Internet connection both at home and at work, but where else do you like to use your computer? If you're used to working on documents on your deck, or while you're at a restaurant for lunch, or in your car, you won't be able to access your cloud-based documents and applications—unless you have a strong Internet connection at all those locations, of course. A lot of what's nice about portable computing becomes problematic when you're depending on web-based applications.

note Some web-based applications are now being designed to work on your desktop when you're not connected to the Internet. Witness Google Gears, a technology that turns Google's web-based applications into locally run applications.

Doesn't Work Well with Low-Speed Connections

Similarly, a low-speed Internet connection, such as that found with dial-up services, makes cloud computing painful at best and often impossible. Web-based apps often require a lot of bandwidth to download, as do large documents. If you're laboring with a low-speed dial-up connection, it might take seemingly forever just to change from page to page in a document, let alone launch a feature-rich cloud service.

In other words, cloud computing isn't for the slow or broadband-impaired.

Can Be Slow

Even on a fast connection, web-based applications can sometimes be slower than accessing a similar software program on your desktop PC. That's because everything about the program, from the interface to the document you're working on, has to be sent back and forth from your computer to the computers in the cloud. If the cloud servers happen to be backed up at that moment, or if the Internet is having a slow day, you won't get the instantaneous access you're used to with desktop apps.

Features Might Be Limited

This particular disadvantage is bound to change, but today many web-based applications simply aren't as full-featured as their desktop-based brethren. Compare, for example, the feature set of Google Presentations with that of Microsoft PowerPoint; there's just a lot more you can do with PowerPoint than you can with Google's web-based offering. The basics are similar, but the cloud application lacks many of PowerPoint's advanced features.

So if you're an advanced user, you might not want to leap into the cloud computing waters just yet. That said, many web-based apps add more advanced features over time. This has certainly been the case with Google Docs and Spreadsheets, both of which started out somewhat crippled but later added many of the more niche functions found on Microsoft Word and Excel. Still, you need to look at the features before you make the move. Make sure that the cloud-based application can do everything you need it to do before you give up on your traditional software.

Stored Data Might Not Be Secure

With cloud computing, all your data is stored on the cloud. That's all well and good, but how secure is the cloud? Can other, unauthorized users gain access to your confidential data?

These are all important questions, and well worth further examination. To that end, read ahead to the "The Security Conscious" section later in this chapter, where we examine just how safe your data is in the cloud.

If the Cloud Loses Your Data, You're Screwed

I can't put it any more delicately. Theoretically, data stored in the cloud is unusually safe, replicated across multiple machines. But on the off chance that your data does go missing, you have no physical or local backup. (Unless you methodically download all your cloud documents to your own desktop, of course—which few users do.) Put simply, relying the cloud puts you at risk if the cloud lets you down.

Who Benefits from Cloud Computing?

Let's face it, cloud computing isn't for everyone. What types of users, then, are best suited for cloud computing—and which aren't?

Collaborators

If you often collaborate with others on group projects, you're an ideal candidate for cloud computing. The ability to share and edit documents in real time between multiple users is one of the primary benefits of web-based applications; it makes collaborating easy and even fun.

Suppose, for example, that you're in charge of an upcoming presentation to the senior management of your company. You need to work with the heads of your company's various departments, which happen to be based in a half-dozen locations. Given everyone's busy schedules, it's tough enough to schedule a group conference call. How in the world can all of you get together to create a cohesive presentation?

The solution, in this instance, is to use a web-based presentation program, such as Google Presentations. You and the department heads can access the main presentation document at your leisure. The changes one person makes are automatically visible when the other collaborators access the document. In fact, more than one of you can edit the document at the same time, with each of your changes happening in real time. Collaborating with a web-based application is both more convenient and faster than trying to assemble everyone's pieces into a single document managed by one member of the team.

This type of collaboration isn't limited to the corporate world. I like the way families and communities use web-based scheduling programs, such as Google Calendar, to manage their busy schedules. On a personal note, my wife and I share a single Google calendar; when she adds an item to the calendar, it automatically shows up on the version that I see. It makes it easy for the two of us to keep our schedules in sync.

Similarly, community groups and sports teams can use web-based calendars to alert their members of upcoming activities. If authorized, group or team members can add their own items to the calendar, helping the entire group plan around individual conflicts.

note I like the story of how one bride used Google Spreadsheets to manage her upcoming wedding. She initially gave access to both her mother and mother-in-law so that they could add or edit elements on her wedding to-do list. It worked fine until her future mother-in-law did a little too much editing to the items the bride had added. The bride ultimately responded by rescinding her mother-in-law's access to the shared spreadsheet!

Road Warriors

Another prime candidate for cloud computing is the road warrior. When you work at one office today, at home the next day, and in another city the next, it's tough to keep track of all your documents and applications. You may end up with one version of a document on your work PC, another on your laptop, and a third on your home PC—and that's if you remember to copy that document and take it with you from one location to the next.

Far better, therefore, if you can access a single version of your document from any location. When you're in the office, you log in to your web-based app and access your stored document. Go home and use your web browser to access the very same app and document via the Internet. Travel to another city and the same application and document are still available to you.

With cloud computing, you don't have to remember which document is where, or to bring a copy of a document with you. You don't even have to worry about whether a particular application is installed on all your PCs. Because the apps and docs you use are stored on the web and accessible wherever you have an Internet connection, versioning and compatibility simply aren't issues. It's the same application and the same document wherever you go.

Could life get any easier?

Cost-Conscious Users

Another group of users who should gravitate to cloud computing are those who are cost conscious. With cloud computing you can save money on both your hardware and software.

Hardware-wise, there's no need to invest in large hard disks or super-fast CPUs. Because everything is stored and run from the web, you can cut costs by buying a less fully featured PC—without sacrificing anything in the way of performance.

You can save just as much—if not more—when it comes to software. Instead of laying out big bucks for the latest version of Microsoft Office, you can use Google's versions of these apps (Google Docs, Spreadsheets, and Presentations) for zero expenditure. That's right, these web-based applications—and many more from other companies—are completely free to use. When your budget is tight, free is a lot better than the hundreds or thousands of dollars you might spend otherwise.

This is why many universities are abandoning Microsoft and turning instead to Google's suite of online applications. Money is always tight on college campuses, and a few hundred dollars savings per student adds up quickly. As long as the web-based application does everything you need that a traditional software program does, why not use the free solution?

Cost-Conscious IT Departments

Many corporate IT departments are also becoming enamored of the cloud computing model. Although they might appreciate the software savings we just discussed, for them bigger savings result from having to buy fewer central servers.

You see, on a corporate network much of the computing takes place on the servers centrally located on the organization's network. When users need more computing power, more servers need to be purchased.

This need for more computing power becomes less of an issue when the organization embraces cloud computing. Instead of purchasing a new server, the IT staff just redirects the computing request out to the cloud. The servers that comprise the cloud have plenty of capacity to handle the organization's increased needs, without the IT staff having to spend a single dime on new hardware.

Users with Increasing Needs

Hardware-based cost savings also apply to individual computer users. Need more hard disk space to store all your digital photos and MP3 files? You could purchase a new external hard drive, or you could utilize lower-cost (or free) cloud storage instead. Having trouble running the latest version of your favorite software program because it's power hungry? Abandon that power-sapping program and use a less-demanding web-based app instead. Need more computing power to tackle a particularly vexing problem? Use the power of the cloud, where thousands of computers are at your disposal.

In the old days, the only solution to increased needs was to purchase more powerful hardware. With cloud computing, the solution is in the cloud—which saves you money.

Who Shouldn't Be Using Cloud Computing?

Now let's look at the flip side of the coin. If cloud computing isn't for everyone, who isn't it for?

The Internet-Impaired

Because cloud computing is based on the Internet cloud and depends on Internet access, if you don't have Internet access, you're out of luck. Without Internet access, you can't run web-based applications or open documents stored on the web. Users without readily available Internet access simply shouldn't be considering a switch to cloud-based computing—until they get Internet access, that is.

The same goes if you have slow Internet access, like that found with dial-up Internet connections. A slow connection isn't much better than none at all when accessing big apps and docs on the web. It takes a long time to download these apps and docs, and that waiting time becomes intolerable on anything less than a broadband connection.

Offline Workers

Along the same lines, anyone who consistently works offline in a non-Internet-enabled environment probably isn't the ideal candidate for cloud computing. That means anyone who works out of their vehicle, anyone who works in an office without Internet access, anyone who works at home without Internet access, and anyone who travels from office to office without guarantee of an Internet connection. No Internet, no cloud computing—it's that simple.

The Security Conscious

Today, we think that cloud computing is safe—but we can't guarantee that. It's certainly possible that cloud systems can be hacked and cloud-based documents accessed by unauthorized users; it's also possible that your data could be snagged during transmission between your computer and the cloud. It may be unlikely, but it can happen.

caution Similarly, I wouldn't trust the cloud to be the sole repository for any of my documents. It may be a belt-and-suspenders approach, but if a document is truly essential, I download a copy of it to my computer's hard drive before I sign off from any web-based application. Better to be safe than sorry.

If your documents are confidential, you probably don't want to trust them with cloud computing just yet. Just as you wouldn't transmit confidential documents over a public Wi-Fi network, you shouldn't upload and store your documents on a cloud computing network with questionable security. When security matters, don't take chances.

Anyone Married to Existing Applications

Today, here's probably the most important reason not to sign up for a web-based application: You use Microsoft Office. That's right, many web-based applications are not completely compatible with Microsoft's file formats. This means it might be difficult if not impossible to open your Word or Excel docs with your web-based app—and vice versa.

If you or your organization is a dyed-in-the-wool Microsoft shop, the move to a web-based application will be a tough one. Make sure that your docs can convert, or that the web-based app can read and write in Microsoft's native formats. If not, it might be more trouble to migrate than it's worth.

There's a similar issue, of course, if you're sharing documents with others who use Microsoft software. If you use an online app, can you save your documents in a format that your Microsoft-equipped friends and colleagues can read? It's a real issue, and one that keeps Microsoft on top of the software pile.

Bottom line: Try before you switch. If your web-based docs aren't fully compatible with Microsoft programs, it might be best to remain a Microsoft shop.

DARK CLOUDS: BARRIERS TO USING WEB-BASED APPLICATIONS

As discussed earlier in this chapter, there are some disadvantages to cloud computing, as we know it today. These disadvantages present significant barriers to the widespread adoption of cloud computing technology—and could, if left unresolved, kill the concept completely.

What are these barriers to adopting web-based applications? They fall into several general groups:

- **Technical issues**. Establishing a cloud computing system is a technical challenge. Hundreds or thousands of individual computers or servers have to be purchased or otherwise commandeered, linked together, and managed. In addition, feature-rich web-based software has to be developed, and served to users with 24/7 uptime. All of this takes significant resources, which smaller companies might not possess.

- **Business model issues**. Given the expense inherent in building a cloud computing system and developing web-based applications, how do companies make money offering cloud computing services? Right now, Google is supplying its cloud services free of charge, which is a difficult way to generate revenue. Even if a company can charge for its cloud services and storage, how should those services be priced? Making money off of any new technology is a vexing issue, but particularly so with technology that literally exists within a cloud.

- **Internet issues**. Because cloud computing is viable only when users have constant access to high-speed Internet connections, the unfortunate fact that the United States is behind the curve in broadband access could be a major stumbling point. That's right, the United States falls well behind other Western nations in the deployment of high-speed Internet access. If enough Americans can't access web-based applications, the entire concept of cloud computing might be doomed.

- **Security issues**. Some feel as if this is a false issue, but I'm not so sure. How secure is cloud storage? If you save your web-based document in a cloud system, are you guaranteed that your document will still be there when you need it—and that it won't be accessed by unauthorized users? Whereas cloud computing companies say their systems are safe and secure, other companies touting data security (such as major retailers and credit card companies) have been victims of data theft. What makes cloud storage more secure?

- **Compatibility issues**. Let's face it, if everyone in your company uses Microsoft Word, you're going to use Microsoft Word, too. Switching platforms is difficult at best, and if web-based applications aren't fully compatible with Microsoft's existing file formats, the move to cloud computing simply won't happen.

- **Social issues**. Finally, there's the big issue of whether the computing public is ready to put its trust in applications and documents that they don't physically "own." There's a security blanket effect to knowing that your apps and docs physically reside on your computer, right there, that you can reach out and touch with your own hands. Knowing that your docs are stored somewhere out in the "cloud" imparts a less fuzzy feeling. Many users might not trust something they can't see or touch. Ceding ownership and control of one's resources requires a major shift in the way we think about computing. It's as big a change as the shift from client/server to desktop computing in the 1980s.

Let's face it, cloud computing is a disruptive technology. Many users and organizations will be slow to change, and many existing software and hardware companies will be downright hostile to the concept. It's interesting that Microsoft has finally embraced cloud computing, in its Live Mesh initiative. After all, it has perhaps the most to lose in the computer industry from the shift from the desktop to the cloud. In a world where Microsoft owns the desktop, there's no guarantee that it'll own the cloud—which might be reason enough for Microsoft competitors to go full-bore with the new technology.

3

Developing Cloud Services

M ost of us approach cloud computing from a user's perspective, focusing on those web-based applications that owe their existence to the cloud. But cloud computing also offers a lot to software developers, who can now develop web-based applications that take advantage of the power and reach of cloud computing.

To this end, many prominent companies—including Amazon.com and Google—are devoting significant resources to cloud services development tools. Read on to learn more about what's available—and what's coming.

Why Develop Web-Based Applications?

The needs of a typical IT department are daunting: They must deliver adequate computing power and data storage to all users within the company. This must be done, of course, within a set budget, and there is the rub; to meet peak needs or to add capacity for new users can often send an IT budget soaring.

For most companies, it is not financially prudent to add capacity that will be used only a small percentage of the time. What the IT department needs is a way to increase capacity or add capabilities without investing in new servers and networking gear, or licensing new software. It is to this need that cloud computing speaks.

Cloud services, in the form of centralized web-based applications, also appeal to the IT professional. One instance of an application hosted in the cloud is cheaper and easier to manage than individual copies of similar software installed on each user's desktop PC. Upgrading a cloud app only has to be done one time, where upgrading traditional software has to be done for each PC on which that software is installed. Then, of course, we have the promise of cloud-enabled collaboration, which just can't be done with traditional desktop apps.

The advantages of cloud services development are particularly notable to smaller businesses, who otherwise wouldn't have the budget or resources to develop large-scale applications. By hosting locally developed web applications within the cloud, the small business avoids the cost of purchasing expensive hardware to host similar software.

Let's face it, most small companies don't have the staff, resources, hardware, or budget to develop and maintain their own applications, or to deal with the rigors of maintaining secure environments. Although they could outsource their software development and hosting, moving those applications to the cloud, companies don't have to invest in locally hosted systems, freeing up their staff and resources to focus on the day-to-day running of their own businesses.

In short, there's a lot to be gained by investing in cloud services development. A company that develops its own web-based applications gains functionality while reducing expenses. The combined power of the cloud is accompanied by lower software purchase and management costs.

The Pros and Cons of Cloud Service Development

Why would you choose to develop new applications using the cloud services model? There are several good reasons to do—and a few reasons to be, perhaps, a bit more cautious.

Advantages of Cloud Development

One of the underlying advantages of cloud development is that of economy of scale. By taking advantage of the infrastructure provided by a cloud computing vendor, a developer can offer better, cheaper, and more reliable applications than is possible within a single enterprise. The application can utilize the full resources of the cloud, if needed—without requiring a company to invest in similar physical resources.

Speaking of cost, because cloud services follow the one-to-many model, cost is significantly reduced over individual desktop program deployment. Instead of purchasing or licensing physical copies of software programs (one for each desktop), cloud applications are typically "rented," priced on a per-user basis. It's more of a subscription model than an asset purchase (and subsequent depreciation) model, which means there's less up-front investment and a more predictable monthly expense stream.

IT departments like cloud applications because all management activities are managed from a central location rather than from individual sites or workstations. This enables IT staff to access applications remotely via the web. There's also the advantage of quickly outfitting users with the software they need (known as "rapid provisioning), and adding more computing resources as more users tax the system (automatic scaling). When you need more storage space or bandwidth, companies can just add another virtual server from the cloud. It's a lot easier than purchasing, installing, and configuring a new server in their data center.

For developers, it's also easier to upgrade a cloud application than with traditional desktop software. Application features can be quickly and easily updated by upgrading the centralized application, instead of manually upgrading individual applications located on each and every desktop PC in the organization. With a cloud service, a single change affects every user running the application, which greatly reduces the developer's workload.

Disadvantages of Cloud Development

Perhaps the biggest perceived disadvantage of cloud development is the same one that plagues all web-based applications: Is it secure? Web-based applications have long been considered potential security risks. For this reason, many businesses prefer to keep their applications, data, and IT operations under their own control.

That said, there have been few instances of data loss with cloud-hosted applications and storage. It could even be argued that a large cloud hosting operation is likely to have better data security and redundancy tools than the average enterprise. In any case, however, even the perceived security danger from hosting critical data and services offsite might discourage some companies from going this route.

> **note** Amazon says that they've addressed the causes of that system failure by placing instances of applications in multiple locations and by assigning elastic IP addresses specially designed for cloud computing.

Another potential disadvantage is what happens if the cloud computing host goes offline. Although most companies say this isn't possible, it has happened. Amazon's EC2 service suffered a massive outage on February 15, 2008, that wiped out some customer application data. (The outage was caused by a software deployment that erroneously terminated an unknown number of user instances.) For clients expecting a safe and secure platform, having that platform go down and your data disappear is a somewhat rude awakening. And, if a company relies on a third-party cloud platform to host all of its data with no other physical backup, that data can be at risk.

Types of Cloud Service Development

The concept of cloud services development encompasses several different types of development. Let's look at the different ways a company can use cloud computing to develop its own business applications.

Software as a Service

Software as a service, or SaaS, is probably the most common type of cloud service development. With SaaS, a single application is delivered to thousands of users from the vendor's servers. Customers don't pay for owning the software; rather, they pay for using it. Users access an application via an API accessible over the web.

Each organization served by the vendor is called a tenant, and this type of arrangement is called a multitenant architecture. The vendor's servers are *virtually partitioned* so that each organization works with a customized virtual application instance.

For customers, SaaS requires no upfront investment in servers or software licensing. For the application developer, there is only one application to maintain for multiple clients.

> **note** An API (application development interface) is an interface that enables a remote program to communicate or use the resources of another program or service.

Many different types of companies are developing applications using the SaaS model. Perhaps the best-known SaaS applications are those offered by Google to its consumer base.

Platform as a Service

In this variation of SaaS, the development environment is offered as a service. The developer uses the "building blocks" of the vendor's development environment to create his own custom application. It's kind of like creating an application using Legos; building the app is made easier by use of these predefined blocks of code, even if the resulting app is somewhat constrained by the types of code blocks available.

Web Services

A web service is an application that operates over a network—typically, over the Internet. Most typically, a web service is an API that can be accessed over the Internet. The service is then executed on a remote system that hosts the requested services.

This type of web API lets developers exploit shared functionality over the Internet, rather than deliver their own full-blown applications. The result is a customized web-based application where a large hunk of that application is delivered by a third party, thus easing development and bandwidth demands for the custom program.

A good example of web services are the "mashups" created by users of the Google Maps API. With these custom apps, the data that feeds the map is provided by the developer, where the engine that creates the map itself is provided by Google. The developer doesn't have to code or serve a map application; all he has to do is hook into Google's web API.

As you might suspect, the advantages of web services include faster (and lower-cost) application development, leaner applications, and reduced storage and bandwidth demands.

In essence, web services keep developers from having to reinvent the wheel every time they develop a new application. By reusing code from the web services provider, they get a jump-start on the development of their own applications.

On-Demand Computing

As the name implies, on-demand computing packages computer resources (processing, storage, and so forth) as a metered service similar to that of a public utility. In this model, customers pay for as much or as little processing and storage as they need.

> **note** On-demand computing is also known as utility computing.

Companies that have large demand peaks followed by much lower normal usage periods particularly benefit from utility computing. The company pays more for their peak usage, of course, but their bills rapidly decline when the peak ends and normal usage patterns resume.

> **note** Companies offering on-demand computing and storage today include Amazon, IBM, Sun, and others.

Clients of on-demand computing services essentially use these services as off-site virtual servers. Instead of investing in their own physical infrastructure, a company operates on a pay-as-you-go plan with a cloud services provider.

On-demand computing itself is not a new concept, but has acquired new life thanks to cloud computing. In previous years, on-demand computing was provided from a single server via some sort of time-sharing arrangement. Today, the service is based on large grids of computers operating as a single cloud.

Discovering Cloud Services Development Services and Tools

As you're aware, cloud computing is at an early stage of its development. This can be seen by observing the large number of small and start-up companies offering cloud development tools. In a more established industry, the smaller players eventually fall by the wayside as larger companies take center stage.

That said, cloud services development services and tools are offered by a variety of companies, both large and small. The most basic offerings provide cloud-based hosting for applications developed from scratch. The more fully featured offerings include development tools and pre-built applications that developers can use as the building blocks for their own unique web-based applications.

So let's settle back and take a look at who is offering what in terms of cloud service development. It's an interesting mix of companies and services.

Amazon

That's right, Amazon, one of the largest retailers on the Internet, is also one of the primary providers of cloud development services. Think of it this way: Amazon has spent a lot of time and money setting up a multitude of servers to service its popular website, and is making those vast hardware resources available for all developers to use.

The service in question is called the Elastic Compute Cloud, also known as EC2. This is a commercial web service that allows developers and companies to rent capacity on Amazon's proprietary cloud of servers—

note For more information about Amazon Web Services, go to aws.amazon.com.

which happens to be one of the biggest server farms in the world. EC2 enables scalable deployment of applications by letting customers request a set number of virtual machines, onto which they can load any application of their choice. Thus, customers can create, launch, and terminate server instances on demand, creating a truly "elastic" operation.

Amazon's service lets customers choose from three sizes of virtual servers:

- Small, which offers the equivalent of a system with 1.7GB of memory, 160GB of storage, and one virtual 32-bit core processor
- Large, which offers the equivalent of a system with 7.5GB of memory, 850GB of storage, and two 64-bit virtual core processors
- Extra large, which offers the equivalent of a system with 15GB of memory, 1.7TB of storage, and four virtual 64-bit core processors

In other words, you pick the size and power you want for your virtual server, and Amazon does the rest.

EC2 is just part of Amazon's Web Services (AWS) set of offerings, which provides developers with direct access to Amazon's software and machines. By tapping into the computing power that Amazon has already constructed, developers can build reliable, powerful, and low-cost web-based applications. Amazon provides the cloud (and access to it), and developers provide the rest. They pay only for the computing power that they use.

AWS is perhaps the most popular cloud computing service to date. Amazon claims a market of more than 330,000 customers—a combination of developers, start-ups, and established companies.

Google App Engine

Google is a leader in web-based applications, so it's not surprising that the company also offers cloud development services. These services come in the form of the Google App Engine, which enables developers to build their own web applications utilizing the same infrastructure that powers Google's powerful applications.

The Google App Engine provides a fully integrated application environment. Using Google's development tools and computing cloud, App Engine applications are easy to build, easy to maintain, and easy to scale. All you have to do is develop your application (using Google's APIs and the Python programming language) and upload it to the App Engine cloud; from there, it's ready to serve your users.

note For more information about the Google App Engine, go to code.google.com/appengine/.

As you might suspect, Google offers a robust cloud development environment. It includes the following features:

- Dynamic web serving
- Full support for all common web technologies
- Persistent storage with queries, sorting, and transactions
- Automatic scaling and load balancing
- APIs for authenticating users and sending email using Google Accounts

In addition, Google provides a fully featured local development environment that simulates the Google App Engine on any desktop computer.

And here's one of the best things about Google's offering: Unlike most other cloud hosting solutions, Google App Engine is completely free to use—at a basic level, anyway. A free App Engine account gets up to 500MB of storage and enough CPU strength and bandwidth for about 5 million page views a month. If you need more storage, power, or capacity, Google intends to offer additional resources (for a charge) in the near future.

IBM

It's not surprising, given the company's strength in enterprise-level computer hardware, that IBM is offering a cloud computing solution. The company is targeting small- and medium-sized businesses with a suite of cloud-based on-demand services via its Blue Cloud initiative.

Blue Cloud is a series of cloud computing offerings that enables enterprises to distribute their computing needs across a globally accessible resource grid. One such offering is the Express Advantage suite, which includes data backup and recovery, email continuity and archiving, and data security functionality—some of the more data-intensive processes handled by a typical IT department.

To manage its cloud hardware, IBM provides open source workload-scheduling software called Hadoop, which is based on the MapReduce software used by

Google in its offerings. Also included are PowerVM and Xen virtualization tools, along with IBM's Tivoli data center management software.

note For more information about IBM's Blue Cloud initiative, go to www.ibm.com.

Salesforce.com

Salesforce.com is probably best known for its sales management SaaS, but it's also a leader in cloud computing development. The company's cloud computing architecture is dubbed Force.com. The platform as a

note For more information about Force.com and AppExchange, go to www.salesforce.com.

service is entirely on-demand, running across the Internet. Salesforce provides its own Force.com API and developer's toolkit. Pricing is on a per log-in basis.

Supplementing Force.com is AppExchange, a directory of web-based applications. Developers can use AppExchange applications uploaded by others, share their own applications in the directory, or publish private applications accessible only by authorized companies or clients. Many applications in the AppExchange library are free, and others can be purchased or licensed from the original developers.

Not unexpectedly, most existing AppExchange applications are sales related—sales analysis tools, email marketing systems, financial analysis apps, and so forth. But companies can use the Force.com platform to develop any type of application. In fact, many small businesses have already jumped on the Force.com bandwagon.

For example, an April 2008 article in *PC World* magazine quoted Jonathan Snyder, CTO of Dreambuilder Investments, a 10-person mortgage investment company in New York. "We're a small company," Snyder said, "we don't have the resources to focus on buying servers and developing from scratch. For us, Force.com was really a jump-start."

Other Cloud Services Development Tools

Amazon, Google, IBM, and Salesforce.com aren't the only companies offering tools for cloud services developers. There are also a number of smaller companies working in this space that developers should evaluate, and that end users may eventually become familiar with. These companies include the following:

- 3tera (www.3tera.com), which offers the AppLogic grid operating system and Cloudware architecture for on-demand computing.
- 10gen (www.10gen.com), which provides a platform for developers to build scalable web-based applications.

- Cohesive Flexible Technologies (www.cohesiveft.com), which offers the Elastic Server On-Demand virtual server platform.

- Joyent (www.joyent.com), which delivers the Accelerator scalable on-demand infrastructure for web application developers, as well as the Connector suite of easy-to-use web applications for small businesses.

- Mosso (www.mosso.com), which provides an enterprise-level cloud hosting service with automatic scaling.

- Nirvanix (www.nirvanix.com), which offers a cloud storage platform for developers, as well as Nirvanix Web Services, which provides file management and other common operations via a standards-based API.

- Skytap (www.skytap.com), which provides the Virtual Lab on-demand web-based automation solution that enables developers to build and configure lab environments using pre-configured virtual machines.

- StrikeIron (www.strikeiron.com), which offers the IronCloud cloud-based platform for the delivery of web services, along with various Live Data services that developers can integrate into their own applications.

In addition, Sun Microsystems has an R&D project, dubbed Project Caroline (www.projectcaroline.net), that provides an open source hosting platform for the development and delivery of web-based applications. Access to Project Caroline's grid is free to the general public.

THE MATURITY LEVEL OF CLOUD SERVICES

To understand where the web-based applications we call cloud services stand in the evolution of hosted computer software, we turn to our good friends at Microsoft, who defined four primary maturity levels.

The first level of maturity defines the traditional application service provider (ASP) model of software delivery, and dates back to the 1990s. At this level, each user has his own customized version of the hosted application and runs his own instance of the application on the host server.

The second level of maturity occurs when the vendor hosts a separate instance of the application for each customer. At this level, all instances use the same implementation; the code is not customized for each user, as it is in a level-one application. Instead, user personalization is provided by detailed configuration options within the application itself.

The third level of maturity signals a major change in how the application is hosted. At this level, the vendor runs a single instance of the application that serves every user. A unique user experience is provided via configurable metadata, and authorization and security policies ensure that each user's data is kept separate from that of other users.

At the fourth and final level of maturity, the vendor hosts multiple users on a load-balanced farm of identical instances. Because the number of servers (and instances) can be increased or decreased as necessary to match demand, this type of system is scalable to a large number of users. In addition, patches and upgrades can be rolled out to the entire user base as easily as to a single user. It is to this level that cloud services aspire.

Cloud Computing for Everyone

Cloud Computing for the Family

Now that you know a little bit about how cloud computing works, let's look at how you can make cloud computing work for you. By that I mean real-world examples of how typical users can take advantage of the collaborative features inherent in web-based applications

We'll start our real-world tour of cloud computing by examining how an average family can use web-based applications for various purposes. As you'll see, computing in the cloud can help a family communicate and collaborate—and bring family members closer together.

Centralizing Email Communications

We'll start our tour of cloud computing for families by examining how a typical family can use cloud-based tools to help improve communications between family members. That's right, computing in the cloud can help families improve their communications skills!

The key here is to enable anywhere/anytime access to email. Precloud computing, your email access was via a single computer, which also stored all your email messages. For this purpose, you probably used a program like Microsoft Outlook or Outlook Express, installed on your home computer. If you wanted to check your home email from work, it took a bit of juggling and perhaps the use of your ISP's email access web page. That web page was never in sync with the messages on your home PC, of course, which is just the start of the problems with trying to communicate in this fashion.

A better approach is to use a web-based email service, such as Google's Gmail (mail.google.com), Microsoft's Windows Live Hotmail (mail.live.com), or Yahoo! Mail (mail.yahoo.com). These services place your email inbox in the cloud; you can access it from any computer connected to the Internet. The messages you receive are stored on the web, as are the messages you send, so nothing depends on a single PC.

The joy of using web-based email is that it doesn't matter what PC you use, your messages are always where they should be and they're always in sync. It's easy to check your home email from work, or from anywhere you happen to be—in a coffeehouse, at a hotel, or even in an airport terminal. Use your work PC, your home PC, your notebook PC, or a friend's PC, it doesn't matter; your messages are in the cloud, not on any of those PCs.

Which means, of course, that you can now stay in contact with all your family members wherever you might happen to be. It's easy for your spouse to send you a message even if she isn't sure where you'll be. You can check your web-based email whether you're in the office or on the road. Just make sure you're connected to the Internet, and then open your web browser and log in to the Gmail or

note In this and the next three chapters, we use web-based applications from Google for many of our examples. This isn't an implicit endorsement of Google apps, but rather a recognition that Google provides web-based applications that are both easy to use and completely free—which makes them quite popular with many users.

note Learn more about web-based email programs in Chapter 18, "Collaborating via Web-Based Communications Tools."

Windows Live Hotmail or Yahoo! Mail website. Go to your inbox and you'll find your spouse's message; reply as necessary and await your spouse's response. Even if you change locations or computers, your spouse's message remains in your inbox, and your reply remains in your sent messages folder.

Collaborating on Schedules

Of course, a lot of family communication concerns schedules. Are we free on Friday night? When is Junior's next soccer game? When is Amber's dentist appointment? When is the dishwasher repair guy coming? Are we free to attend the youngest boy's choir concert at school? When are we all free to take our summer vacation?

The bigger your family, the busier things get—and the more difficult it is to keep everybody's activities straight. Although you could try to keep a paper-based schedule or calendar, it's tough to keep such a thing completely up-to-date—and, of course, you can't consult it when you're not at home.

A better solution is to use a web-based calendar, such as Google Calendar (calendar.google.com) or Yahoo! Calendar (calendar.yahoo.com). Not only is such a calendar accessible to anyone, anywhere, any time over the web, it can also be configured so that everyone in your family can add their own events. When your spouse adds her Thursday evening book group meeting to the calendar, that scheduled event automatically appears on your version of the calendar, as well as what all the other members of your family see.

All you have to do is create a public calendar and authorize access for all the members of your family. Then, when they log in to the calendar site, they see all currently scheduled events and can add new events of their own. And, when you go to add an event, you'll quickly see whether that day and time are free or busy. At that point, it's your call whether you add a conflicting appointment or reschedule the event you wanted to add.

Another great thing about web-based calendars is that you can access your schedule from anywhere. At the office and want to know whether you can work late on Thursday night? Just log in to your web-based calendar and see whether that time is free. On the road and want to see when the next PTA meeting is? Just log in to the

note On a personal note, my wife and I have used a joint Google Calendar for more than a year now. It helped us keep our busy schedules straight when we were just dating and trying to juggle two separate lives in two different states; it's even more useful now that we're married (and living in the same state!).

Internet and use your web browser to see what the calendar says. And any changes you make, from wherever you are, are registered in the cloud; your other family members immediately see the latest version of the calendar.

note Learn more about web-based calendars in Chapter 7, "Collaborating on Calendars, Schedules, and Task Management."

Collaborating on Grocery Lists

Here's one you might not have thought of. If you're part of a busy family where both spouses work, you might not be able to manually coordinate your grocery lists. Your spouse might need shampoo, but if she didn't tell you before you left for work, you can stop at the grocery and get everything but what your spouse needs. Likewise if you have a craving for cookies and cream ice cream; if your spouse doesn't know this, your craving will go unfulfilled the next time she stops at the supermarket.

The solution here is to use a web-based word processing program to manage your joint grocery lists. Use a program like Google Docs (docs.google.com) to create a document, and then authorize access for both you and your spouse. Enter the items you need onto the list, one line at a time, and have your spouse do the same.

Keep the list going for the week or so it takes you to get to the grocery, opening your web browser and adding new items as they occur to you, whenever and wherever they occur to you (as long as you have web access, of course). At the end of the week, when you're ready to go to the supermarket, connect to the Internet and print out a copy of your grocery list on your home or office printer. It's that simple.

Of course, you don't have to limit access to your grocery list to just you and your spouse. Many families also authorize their children to access their online lists, thus making everyone in the family happy—and inflating your grocery bill with all sorts of unhealthful snack foods. (But at least everyone will be happy!)

Collaborating on To-Do Lists

A grocery list is just one type of to-do list. If you have a lot of household chores and repairs, it's likely that you have a larger to-do list for your household. And, if your household is like mine, that list grows every day!

note Learn more about web-based word processing applications in Chapter 11, "Collaborating on Word Processing."

You and your spouse can collaborate on your to-do list by using a web-based word processing application, as we just discussed, or you can use a dedicated web-based planning program. These

note Learn more about web-based planning programs in Chapter 7.

applications, such as Zoho Planner (planner.zoho.com) let you create multiple to-do lists on the web, which you and your spouse can both add to from any computer, at any time. You can even set email reminders to refresh your memory when a task is due. Add your tasks one at a time, and then mark them off as they're completed.

If these applications are too advanced for your needs, consider using a simpler web-based to-do list application. These applications, such as Remember the Milk (www.rememberthemilk.com) and Ta-da List (www.tadalist.com), operate more like a simple notepad-based list. Some even let you add tasks via email or access the list when you're on the go with your mobile phone.

Collaborating on Household Budgets

If you're like me, you don't like surprises—especially financial ones. I like to keep a rather tight cash flow budget for my family, so that I know what's coming in and what's going out on a weekly basis. Problems occur when my wife has a big expense that I didn't know about—and didn't budget for.

You can minimize these types of unwelcome surprises by collaborating with your spouse on your household budget. This is easy enough to do when you use a web-based spreadsheet program, such as Google Spreadsheets (part of the Google Docs suite, at docs.google.com), to create your budget; you and your spouse can then enter budget items separately, when it's convenient for both of you.

Remember an upcoming expenditure while you're sitting in a meeting at work? Just go online and add the expense to your web-based budget. Find out about a necessary repair when you're watching TV? Just walk over to your home PC, log in to the web-based spreadsheet, and enter that expense. Budgets get a lot easier when you can update them any time and anywhere— and when both spouses can do so.

Of course, budget collaboration can also be interactive. Perhaps you see a new flat-screen TV in your future, and enter that item into your web-based budget. Your spouse might disagree about the item's importance or cost. She can just as easily go online and lower the budget for that item—or delete it completely!

So just because you can put together a
budget online doesn't mean you still don't
have to talk about it. Remember that collaboration sometimes involves compro-
mise.

note Learn more about
web-based spread-
sheet applications in Chapter 11.

Collaborating on Contact Lists

You have your friends, your spouse has her friends, and both of you have
business contacts and acquaintances that you need to keep track of—even if
you only reach out to them once a year or so. If your family is like mine, this
describes the list we use for our annual holiday cards, which for us
approaches a hundred names long.

Managing your family's contact list isn't always easy. Yes, you have your
most-contacted contacts stored in Microsoft Outlook or some similar program,
but that list of names exists only on one computer. Your contacts are on your
PC, your spouse's contacts are on her PC, and your lists of work contacts are
probably on your work computers. How do you merge and manage all these
names—in time to address and mail your cards before the holidays?

A good solution for managing contacts from multiple family members is to
use a web-based program for contact management. There are few different
ways to approach this.

First, you can use your web-based email program (Gmail, Yahoo! Mail, and so
on) as a contact management program. All of these programs let you create
and store complete information about your contacts—email address, postal
address, phone number, and so forth. The only problem with using this
approach, however, is that both you and your spouse have to use the same
email program and the same email address. So, it might not work for you.

A more robust and individualized solution is to use a dedicated web-based
contact management program. Some of these programs, such as MyEvents
(www.myevents.com) are targeted at home users and ideal for holiday card
lists; other programs, such as Highrise (www.highrisehq.com) will manage
your holiday card list and do a lot more. These latter programs include the
robust customer resource management (CRM) features needed for business
and sales force management.

Whichever type of program you decide to use (or, perhaps, you just use a web-
based spreadsheet program, with one row per contact), you need to authorize
access for both you and your spouse. This way you can both import your
existing Outlook or Windows Address Book contacts, as well as add new

names when and where they come up. Maybe you meet somebody new when you're on a business trip, or your spouse runs into an old friend at the local coffeehouse. All either of you need to do is log onto your web-based application from wherever you are and add the new person's name and contact info. Then, when it comes holiday time, one of you accesses the main list and prints it out or uses it to print mailing labels. Voilà! Your holiday list is finished.

> **note** Learn more about web-based contact management applications in Chapter 9, "Collaborating on Contact Management."

Collaborating on School Projects

You and your spouse aren't the only family members who can benefit from the collaborative nature of web-based applications. Consider your school-aged children, and all the school projects they have to do. Many of these projects are group projects, and there's no easier way to collaborate on a group project than to use web-based applications.

Let's say that little Timmy is assigned to a group of students that has to put together a presentation on Mark Twain. These days, most grade school students know how to use Microsoft PowerPoint, so something similar is required for the final presentation. Instead of driving your kids around to each others' houses, they can collaborate over the web from their own homes, saving you time and gasoline.

There are several decent web-based presentation programs, but one of the most popular (probably because it's free) is Google Presentations, part of the Google Docs suite of programs (docs.google.com). It's easy for each member of the team to add to the presentation as they see fit. When one member adds a new slide, other team members see that slide immediately on their own computer screens.

To facilitate communication during the span of the project, your kids can use a web-based email program, such as Gmail, to send messages back and forth from their own computers. Even better, sign them up to an instant messaging service, such as AOL Instant Messenger (www.aim.com) or Yahoo! Messenger (messenger.yahoo.com), so that they can text each other in real time.

If the project is particularly complicated, it might help for the kids to coordinate their schedules for all the pieces and parts. Basic project management can be accomplished in a web-based calendar program, such as Google Calendar (calendar.google.com), or in a simple planner program, such as

Zoho Planner (planner.zoho.com). For more complicated projects with a lot of individual tasks, consider using a dedicated project management application, such as Basecamp (www.basecamphq.com). Whatever application they use, the kids should break their project down into all its component parts, and assign each part to an individual—along with a due date.

note Learn more about web-based presentation programs in Chapter 14, "Collaborating on Presentations." Learn more about web-based email and instant messaging in Chapter 18, "Collaborating via Web-Based Collaboration Tools." And learn more about web-based project management tools in Chapter 10, "Collaborating on Project Management."

Of course, most projects require a written component in addition to the live presentation. For this, sign the kids up to web-based word processing program. If they're already using Google Presentations, they might as well use Google Docs for this purpose. Again, each of the students can write their own sections online and have the master document updated automatically and immediately. Just make sure one of the kids remembers to print out the report when it's done!

When it comes time to give the presentation, the students have a few options. If they have a live Internet connection in the classroom, they might as well use Google Presentations to display the final presentation. If not, they can save the Google presentation in PPT format, and use the classroom's copy of PowerPoint to give the live show.

Sharing Family Photos

Here's one thing most families have lots of: photographs. In today's digital world, the photographs are likely digital ones, capable of being shared via email or uploaded to the web.

When you have photos you want to share with a lot of family and friends, the best course of action is to use a web-based photo sharing service. There are lots of these sites available, from noncommercial sites like Flickr (www.flickr.com) to sites that like to sell you prints and other products, such as Shutterfly (www.shutterfly.com). Any of these sites let you create your own online photo albums and then upload your digital photos to these albums. You then send the album's URL to your friends and family, and they can view all your photos online—either one at a time or in an online photo slideshow.

Many of these sites go the next step and let visitors order prints of the photos you upload. (That's how they make money, after all; the photo hosting is typically free.) When your Aunt Edna sees a photo she likes, it's a simple matter to check that photo, click the "order prints" button, provide her credit card number, and have prints made and delivered to her door.

note Learn more about web-based photo-sharing and photo-editing applications in Chapter 16, "Sharing Digital Photographs."

Of course, not every photo you take is a winner. Many digital photos can benefit greatly from simple photo editing. Although some photo sharing sites offer modest photo editing capabilities, you're probably better off using a dedicated web-based photo editing application, such as Adobe's Photoshop Express (www.photoshop.com/express/). These programs not only offer easy-to-use photo editing tools, but also help you manage the photos stored on your own PC. And, because they're based in the cloud, you can access these programs (typically for free) from any PC anywhere you have an Internet connection.

THE COLLABORATIVE FAMILY

In the old days, family life was simpler. Kids had less homework, fewer friends, and fewer activities and commitments. Adults had a work life and a home life, and the two didn't overlap. There were fewer time constraints across the board; you worked or went to school during the day and did family stuff at night and on weekends.

Today, family life is a lot more complicated. Kids have tons of home-work (much of it requiring online research and group collaboration), hundreds of virtual friends located around the globe, and a schedule of activities so full it takes a full-time project manager to keep track of them all. Adults take work home with them and manage home activities at work, thanks to BlackBerries, iPhones, and notebook computers. It's tough to tell when work ends and family time begins. And for all concerned, life is a never-ending series of tasks and commitments and things that have to be done *now*, no exceptions.

All this activity causes time and schedule stress among all the members of your family, from the oldest to the youngest. Although technology can't make any of these tasks go away (and in fact enable some of this hyperactivity), it can help you manage what you're doing. Technology—cloud computing technology in particular—is proving quite useful in helping people keep track of various tasks and activities, and coordinate and collaborate with others to better get things done.

When cloud computing enters the picture, the result is new type of collaborative family environment. Even if individual family members don't have the time (or are never in the same physical location) to have face-to-face conversations, they can still keep in touch via email and instant messaging; they can collaborate on grocery shopping and to-do lists and who knows what all else by using web-based applications. It might not be as ideal as everyone sitting down and talking face to face, but at least you're still in touch—and working together to get your lives in order.

Cloud Computing for the Community

Cloud computing isn't just for home users. It has tremendous benefits for the entire community, from neighborhood groups to sports teams to school organizations. Any time any group of people in the community need to communicate and collaborate, web-based applications are the way to go.

This chapter, therefore, takes a look at a few typical community uses of cloud computing. After examining the web-based approach, it's hard to imagine going back to the old way of doing things.

Communicating Across the Community

Alliteration aside, one of the key components of any community collaboration is
communication. This isn't as easy as it

note Learn more about web-based email programs in Chapter 18, "Collaborating via Web-Based Communication Tools."

sounds, because many community activities are undertaken by people in their
spare time—outside of normal work and home activities. Therefore, they
might be communicating during office hours on their work computer, after
hours on their home computer, or during any spare moment wherever they
may happen to be. That makes using traditional desktop email, such as
Microsoft Outlook or Windows Mail, problematic.

The better solution when communication on community issues is to use a
web-based email program, such as Gmail (mail.google.com), Microsoft
Windows Live Hotmail (mail.live.com), or Yahoo! Mail (mail.yahoo.com).
These programs can be accessed from any computer connected to the Internet.
You use your web browser to send and view email messages hosted on the
web. You can send and receive messages at work, at home, or from wherever
you happen to be. Everything you send and receive is stored in the cloud,
accessible from anywhere at any time.

Some community activists go so far as to create a unique web-based email
account just for their community communications. This way they don't con-
fuse personal emails from those involving their community activities.

Collaborating on Schedules

When it comes to coordinating multiple individuals or families in a community activity, you have your work cut out for you. Whether it's a youth sports
team, community organization, school event, or some community event, trying to line up who's free and who's not on a given evening takes a lot of
effort—unless, that is, you're using web-based scheduling tools.

Sports Team Schedules

Here's one of the most common community activities: youth sports. Maybe your
son is on an intramural football team, or
your daughter is into youth soccer.
Whatever the age, whatever the sport,
there's a lot of activities that need to be

note Learn more about web-based calendar tools in Chapter 7, "Collaborating on Calendars, Schedules, and Task Management."

scheduled—practices, home games, away games, team meetings, you name it. Multiply the number of players (and coaches) on each team times the number of events, and you see the complexity; it gets even worse if you're trying to manage events for an entire league.

How best, then, to juggle all the schedules of so many people and events? The best way is to use a web-based calendar tool, such as Google Calendar (calendar.google.com), Yahoo! Calendar (calendar.yahoo.com), or CalendarHub (www.calendarhub.com). Just create a public calendar and provide the URL to all the team members. After you add all your team activities to the calendar, team members simply have to log in to see what's coming up this week and next.

Also good are dedicated sports team website builders. These sites offer tools designed specifically for sports teams, including home pages complete with schedule, roster, player profiles, box scores, and the like. Most of these services even design your site using your team colors and logo. There are several of these web-based applications, including eteemz (www.eteemz.com), League Athletics (www.leagueathletics.com), LeagueLineup (www.leaguelineup.com), and TeamSnap (www.teamsnap.com). Figure 5.1 shows a typical League Athletics site, for the Lakeville (Minnesota) Baseball Association.

FIGURE 5.1

The Lakeville Baseball Association uses League Athletics to manage its activities on the web.

School Schedules

Web-based calendars are also ideal for keeping track of various school schedules. Whether it's homework assignments for a particular class or a school-wide events schedule, it's easy for a teacher or school to post that schedule on a web-based calendar. Make the calendar public (but make sure only authorized personnel can post new events), and then provide the calendar's URL to all students and parents. Assuming that all families have Internet access (it helps to check this first), there should be no excuse for missed homework or absence from key events.

Community Group Schedules

Any community group can benefit from organizing their activities via a web-based calendar. Want to schedule practices for a community theater production? Announce meetings for your local school board? Organize bingo nights for your church? Any and all of these group activities can easily be managed online, in the cloud, using a web-based calendar.

Event Schedules and Management

You can also use web-based calendars to post dates and schedules for specific public events, such as school plays, or for all events in a given community. Although any web-based calendar program can do this job, as well, some event-specific applications are worth noting.

For example, Zvents (zvents.com) is a web search engine for local events. Upload your event schedule into the Zvents database, and then anyone in your area can find out what's happening in the coming days and weeks. Figure 5.2 shows a typical Zvents community home page. Users can also search for events by type, location, and date.

Also interesting is the suite of event management software from ServiceU (www.serviceu.com). Included in this suite is the EventU application, which offers event, resource, and facility scheduling for organizations small or large.

note Other components of the ServiceU suite include TransactU (registration/payment) and TicketU (online ticketing).

FIGURE 5.2
Searching for local events online with Zvents.

Collaborating on Group Projects and Events

Community groups often have a lot on their plates. Someone has to schedule the next fundraiser, someone else needs to print up flyers, someone else is in charge of recruiting new members...there's just a lot of stuff to do!

How does your community group manage all these activities? In the new world of cloud computing, the best way is with a web-based application—which anyone in the group can access.

Collaborating on To-Do Lists

Let's start with simple task management, in the form of the old-fashioned to-do list. These are web-based lists that multiple group members can access from any web browser. Tasks are entered (complete with due date) and checked off when completed.

Some of the more popular online to-do list applications include Bla-Bla List (www.blablalist.com), Remember the Milk (www.rememberthemilk.com), Ta-da List (www.tadalist.com), Tudu List (www.tudulist.com), and Voo2Do (www.voo2do.com). All of these applications are simple enough for even the most techno-phobic group members to use. Some even let you add new tasks via email or access your lists via mobile phone.

note Learn more about to-do lists and task management programs in Chapter 7.

Collaborating on Task Management

For managing more complex tasks, a simple to-do list application might not cut the mustard. Instead, consider using a web-based task management application that lets you manage the multiple pieces and parts of large projects.

Basic task management can be accomplished with applications such as HiTask (www.hitask.com) and Zoho Planner (planner.zoho.com). For the most complicated projects, consider using a dedicated project management application, such as Basecamp (www.basecamphq.com) or Goplan (www.goplan.com). Whichever option you choose, you must break your project down into all its component tasks, set a due date for each, and then assign each task to a specific group member. Group members can then access the application online from their own computers and update the project with their own individual progress.

Collaborating on Event Management

When you're putting on a big event such as a concert or conference, you have a whole new set of challenges to face. Not only do you have to manage the tasks involved with putting together the event, you also have to handle attendee registration, event marketing, ticket sales, and the like. It's a massive effort—made somewhat easier by web-based event management tools.

With web-based event management applications, the cloud hosts everything you need to schedule and market your events, as well as handle registration, payment, and other important tasks. For example, you can create an online event calendar so that attendees can learn about and sign up for future events via the web; offer web-based event registration and payment; manage requests for hotel rooms,

note Learn more about online project management applications in Chapter 10, "Collaborating on Project Management."

airline flights, and car rentals; and check in attendees live onsite via a notebook PC with Internet connection. Most of these apps also offer detailed task and budget management functions.

note Learn more about online event management in Chapter 8, "Collaborating on Event Management."

These are very robust applications, capable of handling every last detail over the web. Some of the most popular of these apps include Cvent (www.cvent.com), RegOnline (www.regonline.com), and ViewCentral (www.rmkr.com/viewcentral). Unlike some other web-based apps, these aren't free; you have to pay for the power you need to manage the details of your particular event.

Collaborating on Event Marketing

We briefly mentioned event marketing in the previous section. That's because most event management applications also handle basic event marketing.

But when it comes to promoting your community events, you want to go beyond the basics to more creative forms of marketing. For example, you may want to create a brochure or flyer to announce your event. Fine and dandy, but everybody in the group (including all the community bigwigs) wants input on the final piece. This may have been difficult in precloud days, but now you can use a web-based application such as Google Docs (docs.google.com) to create your piece and make it available online for everyone to see and comment on. (Just remember to dole out read-only authorization to these interested parties; you don't want everybody in the group going online and making changes to what you've just created!)

Naturally, you can also use web-based local search sites, such as Zvents (www.zvents.com), to post announcements of your community events. You may even want to use cloud-based social media sites, such as Facebook and MySpace, to promote your event online. And, after the event, you can post pictures of the event on community photo-sharing sites, such as Flickr (www.flickr.com). It's all possible because of the cloud!

Collaborating on Budgets

Every event, small or large, comes with its own set of costs. And with community events, those costs are often managed by a group of people, each responsible for a specific operation or group of operations.

note Learn more about web-based document creation tools in Chapter 11, "Collaborating on Word Processing."

For simple events, you can collaborate on your budget using web-based spreadsheet programs, such as Google Spreadsheets (part of the Google Docs suite, at docs.google.com). Just create a private spreadsheet, authorize access for each member responsible for the budget, and then start adding data online. When everyone has finished entering numbers for their line items, the group member responsible for the entire budget can log on and do her thing.

> **note** Learn more about spreadsheet applications in Chapter 12, "Collaborating on Spreadsheets."

For larger or more complex events, you may want to use the budget function available in most event management programs. You may also want to consider some of the accounting applications in the Salesforce.com AppExchange (www.salesforce.com/appexchange/). Some of these web-based apps are relatively low-priced, which is an attractive asset for most cash-strapped community groups.

VIRTUAL COMMUNITIES IN THE CLOUD

When we think of community organizations, we tend to focus on those groups operating within the confines of a physical community. But not all communities are geographically based; the growth of the Internet has seen the advent of virtual communities, located solely within the cloud.

A virtual community is an assemblage of like-minded individuals, from anywhere in the world, online. Pre-Internet, virtual communities sprung up on online bulletin board systems (BBSs) that were accessible via dial-up connections. In the early 1990s, these communities migrated to the commercial online services provided by America Online, CompuServe, and Prodigy. Then, when the Internet first gained public prominence, even more virtual communities found their home in Usenet newsgroups.

Today, the Internet is synonymous with the web, and almost all virtual communities are web based. Many communities are based in web forums and message boards. Still others coalesce around eBay and other hobbyist-friendly sites.

But the biggest home of virtual communities today are Facebook, MySpace, and other social networking sites. These Web 2.0 sites let like-minded individuals create free-flowing communities around users' personal pages; musicians, celebrities, and even normal individuals all create communities of friends around their Facebook and MySpace pages.

Is a virtual community a real community? It is when there is a constant interchange of thoughts and ideas between group members—which is what happens on a popular Facebook or MySpace page. Community communications don't have to happen face to face; a group can have a discussion that's entirely virtual, thanks to today's cloud-based communications tools. And, to be honest, many online communities are more vibrant than some physical communities. After all, physical proximity doesn't guarantee a commonality in interests or a harmony in dispositions. It might actually be easier to find people you like and have something in common with online than it is in your own local community. That is, perhaps, as good a reason as any to embrace virtual communities—while still supporting your local community, of course.

Cloud Computing for the Corporation

Businesses have been some of the earlier adopters of cloud computing. Companies large and small recognize the cost savings and productivity enhancements of using web-based tools to manage projects, collaborate on documents and presentations, manage enterprisewide contacts and schedules, and the like. Cloud computing lets companies do more with limited budgets.

In addition, web-based applications have proven a boon for telecommuters and road warriors. Instead of being tied to documents and applications hosted on their office desktops, workers can now access what they need from any location—in the office, at home, or on the road.

With all that in mind, let's look at some of the many ways that companies and their employees can use cloud computing.

Managing Schedules

If you work in a large company, you know what a hassle it is to schedule even simple meetings. One person is free on Tuesday at 9:00, but another is out of the office, and yet other attendee is already booked for that time slot. Plus, you're not even sure which meeting room is free at that time. You end up sending a flurry of emails back and forth, trying to find the one spot in everybody's schedules that is free. There has to be a better way.

That better way is web-based scheduling. Everyone places his or her schedule in the cloud, which then enables the meeting's organizer to easily see who's available when. The cloud-based app finds the best time for all involved and schedules the meeting. No more emails, no more phone calls; it all happens automatically, in the cloud.

Here's how it works. Let's suppose you need to schedule a meeting sometime next week with a dozen different attendees. You punch in the details of the meeting and the desired attendees, and the scheduling app finds the first available timeslot when all attendees are free. Alternatively, the app might have to pick a timeslot when the maximum number of people can attend. This kind of "best case scenario" scheduling might be the only way to get your meeting on the calendar in a reasonable period of time.

Web-based scheduling programs let you schedule both in-person meetings and teleconferences with attendees from multiple locations. You're not limited to just those people located in your office; you can work with the schedules of people around the country and even in different firms.

Of course, much of this can be accomplished with simple web-based calendar programs, such as Google Calendar (calendar.google.com) and Yahoo! Calendar (calendar.yahoo.com). To take advantage of the more advanced automatic scheduling features, however, you need to use an industrial strength scheduling application, such as AppointmentQuest (www.appointmentquest.com), hitAppoint (www.hitappoint.com), and Schedulebook (www.schedulebook.com). Naturally, these enterprise-level apps cost more to use than the free web-based calendars; expect to pay anywhere from $20 to $200 subscription fees per month.

note Learn more about web-based scheduling programs in Chapter 7, "Collaborating on Calendars, Schedules, and Task Management."

Managing Contact Lists

Salespeople have to deal with lots and lots of contacts. Not only is their address book full, they need to know when to contact certain clients, when follow-up calls are necessary, what the boss needs them to do today, and the like. This is difficult to do from a simple desktop contact management program, such as Microsoft Outlook, which merely acts as a storehouse for names and contact info. It's also difficult to do when you're on the road and need access to all your contacts.

The solution, of course, is a web-based contact management or customer resource management (CRM) application. These programs are tailored to the needs of a busy salesperson and come complete with features such as activity scheduling, appointment reminders, email templates, and the like.

Among the most popular of these applications are BigContacts (www.bigcontacts.com), Highrise (www.highrisehq.com), and the market-leading Salesforce.com (www.salesforce.com). Many of these apps include additional functions of use to large sales departments, including expense account management, sales activity reports, and various team management features.

Using a web-based contact or CRM application can be as simple or as complex as you make it. You might need nothing more than access to a large list of contacts from any location; that's the simple usage. On the other hand, you might want to customize the program so that you're automatically flagged each day with a list of accounts to contact (and for what purposes). Some communication can even be automated, via the use of scheduled emails.

Imagine the typical day on the road for a traveling salesperson. You wake up in your hotel room, turn on your notebook computer, and log in to the hotel's free wireless Internet connection. Using your web browser, you access the CRM application's website and look at today's list of tasks. You click a button to launch a list of scheduled emails to be sent to selected clients, and then scroll through the list of phone calls you need to make today. If you need more information about a particular client, just click that contact's link. Everything you've entered about that client is stored online and instantly accessible. You can even click a link to view driving directions and a map to the first client you need to visit. And, to see how you're doing against this month's quota, you end the session by creating a detailed sales tracking report.

note Learn more about contact management and CRM programs in Chapter 9, "Collaborating on Contact Management."

Naturally, the more detailed your needs, the more features of the application you'll use. The key is that everything is stored and managed in the cloud so that you—and your sales manager—can access important contact information from anywhere at any time; all you need is an Internet connection.

Managing Projects

Most companies at one point or another have at least one big project going on—the type of project that involves multiple employees from multiple departments and perhaps multiple locations. Projects of this type have tons of individual pieces and parts, each of which dependent on the completion of a previous task. Keeping track of all the individual tasks—who's doing what and when—can take a gargantuan effort.

That effort is made easier with the use of a web-based project management application. Project members can log in from any location to access the project's master file; they can add or delete tasks, mark tasks as complete, enter detailed billing information for individual tasks, and so forth. And because the project is hosted in the cloud, every team member sees the same Gantt or PERT chart and the same list of tasks, instantly updated when any other member makes an edit.

Many project management applications include additional functions useful in the management of group projects. These features may include group to-do lists, web-based file sharing, message boards, time and cost tracking, and so on. And the most robust of these apps lets you manage multiple projects simultaneously; users can schedule their time across multiple projects and make sure they're not doing two things at once.

As you might expect, these are not simple applications; they can't be, given the enormity of many enterprise-level projects. Therefore, they're expensive to license and often difficult to learn how to use. The most popular of these apps include AceProject (www.aceproject.com), Basecamp (www.basecamphq.com), onProject (www.onproject.com), and Project Insight (www.projectinsight.com).

note Learn more about web-based project management in Chapter 10, "Collaborating on Project Management."

Collaborating on Reports

When you work for a larger enterprise, chances are you get to write a lot of reports—and these days, the reports you write are often in collaboration with one or more other employees. For example, you may need to put together a monthly progress report that includes input from the company's marketing, sales, and finance departments. Or perhaps you're preparing a business plan that includes sections from all the company's departments, or a company overview that includes bits and pieces from each and every office location. In short, you need some way to collaborate with other staffers when writing the report.

Fortunately, online collaboration is one of the chief benefits of cloud computing. Instead of emailing Microsoft Word documents across the company, opt instead for a web-based word processing program, such as Google Docs (docs.google.com) or Zoho Writer (writer.zoho.com). With one of these applications, everyone contributing to the report can access the same master document, online and in real time. When someone from one department adds his section to the document, all the other staffers immediately see the update.

The best web-based word processors work in conjunction with full-fledged web-based office suites. Google Docs, for example, encompasses word processing, spreadsheet, and presentation functions. Zoho's suite of apps includes similar word processing, spreadsheet, and presentation functions—as well as a neat little project management module.

Collaborating on a web-based document is surprisingly easy. Most projects start with the team leader creating a new document online and giving it a bit of form—some sort of content and style template. The leader then assigns sections of the report to appropriate individuals, and provides the document URL to each individual. These contributors then work on their own sections of the report, logging in to the master document via their web browsers. When all the individual sections are complete, the project leader then looks at the document as a whole, editing for consistency and making sure that all appropriate data is included.

Most online word processing applications let you embed photos and other graphics; you may also be able to include spreadsheet files as part of the master document. The result is a quality document that reflects the true collaborative nature of the project.

> **note** Learn more about web-based word processors in Chapter 11, "Collaborating on Word Processing."

Collaborating on Marketing Materials

Marketing is another area that benefits from cloud-enabled collaboration. Putting together a catalog requires data from several different departments. For example, effective direct mail campaign benefits from marketing, sales, and fulfillment input. Online PR needs participation from marketing, product, and technical staff.

When it comes to creating marketing materials, perhaps the best approach is to use a combination of web-based applications. Naturally, web-based email facilitates communication between departments; you can also benefit from web-based project management apps, to help keep all the pieces and parts in line.

The marketing materials themselves can be created using web-based word processing applications. This puts the draft materials on the web, for everyone on the team (including appropriate senior management) to see, comment on, and even contribute to. After everyone's had his or her say, you can finalize the document and send it to your printer or website.

Collaborating on Expense Reports

If you spend your company's money, you have to account for it. That's the theory behind the reality of expense reports, the bane of all free-spending employees.

It's not too difficult to create an expense report using your favorite spreadsheet software, but that isn't always the best way to go. The paper or electronic report must then wend its way through your company's various levels of approval: your boss, your boss' boss, the accounting department, the HR department, and who knows how many more people before the accounting folks finally cut you a check.

A better solution for many companies is to put the expense reporting function on the web. Employees from any location can access the website to enter their expenses; it can even be accessed while employees are still traveling, with no need to wait for reimbursement until they get home. Then the web-based expense report gets electronically circulated to everyone who needs to approve it or, more likely, a link to the web-based report is emailed instead. Finally, after the last approval is entered (electronically, of course), the accounting department is notified and a check is cut. No costly paper trail is generated, no documents spend days waiting in someone's inbox, and the entire process is expedited—which means employees get reimbursed faster.

Another benefit of web-based expense management is that you can quickly and easily ensure that all employees follow your company's rules and regulations. Just add your own rulebase into the app's management console, and employees will have to follow your company's policies when entering their expenses.

Some of the most popular enterprise-level web-based expense reporting applications include Concur (www.concur.com), ExpensAble (www.expensable.com), ExpensePoint (www.expensepoint.com), and TimeConsultant (www.timeconsultant.com). Many web-based office management and workforce management applications also include expense reporting modules.

Collaborating on Budgets

While we're on the topic of money, there's no bigger project at many companies than creating next year's budget. Every department is involved, with managers required to submit complete department budgets (the creation of which involves several departmental employees) that are then rolled up by the finance department into a complete company budget. That budget is seldom approved as is, of course, which means adjustments are then rolled back down the line; the departments make the required changes and resubmit their budgets, which are then rolled back up again to the final company budget. It's a long and involved process.

Traditionally, each department works on its own budget spreadsheet, which is then emailed to the finance department for consolidation with those of other departments. Although that's more efficient than moving sheets of greenbar paper around the office, it's not as efficient as it could be.

Cloud computing offers a better approach. Instead of working on separate spreadsheets that are later consolidated, you can use a web-based application to create a single budget document for all departments on the web. Each department head enters his own budget data. The rolled-up budget is then created in real-time. When the big bosses need to slash certain expenditures, those changes are immediately reflected in the sections or pages for each individual department.

This type of online budgeting can be accomplished with a simple web-based spreadsheet, such as Google Spreadsheets (spreadsheets.google.com) or with a dedicated enterprise-level budgeting application, such as Host Budget (www.hostanalytics.com/budgeting-planning-software.html). In addition, many office management and project management applications include budgeting modules, so that may be an option for your particular firm.

note Learn more about web-based spreadsheets in Chapter 12, "Collaborating on Spreadsheets."

Collaborating on Financial Statements

Assembling a monthly or year-end profit-and-loss statement or income statement is like a budget, but from the other side—that is, it requires input from all departments, but it measures what actually happened rather than making a projection.

Given the fast-paced nature of financial reporting these days, the accounting department needs final figures from all relevant department as soon as possible after month-end or year-end close. Instead of waiting for each department to mail or email its results, the entire process is accelerated when each department enters its data directly into a master spreadsheet. Because this spreadsheet is housed on the web, even departments in remote locations can have their data recognized as soon as they enter it.

Although you could use a web-based spreadsheet program, such as Google Spreadsheets, for this task, a better approach might be to invest in a web-based accounting program. For example, Host Consolidator (www.hostanalytics.com/consolidation-reporting.html) bills itself as a web-based financial consolidation, analysis, and reporting application. Authorized individuals can enter appropriate data from any location, using any web browser. Once month-end or year-end data has been entered, the application automatically generates a variety of financial reports, including balance sheet, income statement, cash flow statement, and the like.

Collaborating on Presentations

Every company today sees more than its fair share of PowerPoint presentations. Want to introduce a new product to the sales force? Want to discuss HR hiring trends? Want to present last month's financials to senior management? Then you need to put together a snazzy presentation—and show it from your laptop.

The problem with producing a large presentation is that you often need input from more than one person, department, or office. If you're presenting company financials, for example, you need to get those from each individual department. If you're presenting to your sales force, you might need to assemble product information from multiple divisions. If you're giving an HR presentation, you may require input from the managers of all of your company's physical locations.

> **note** Learn more about web-based presentation programs in Chapter 14, "Collaborating on Presentations."

As with most collaborations of this type, a collaborative presentation is problematic. Let's face it, it's just plain difficult to get everyone involved to submit work on time—and in the proper format. Anyone in charge of such a project has probably already gone bald from tearing his hair out.

Fortunately, cloud computing makes collaborating on presentations a whole lot easier. By creating a single presentation document, you don't have to worry about consolidating information from multiple documents. And because that document is located in the cloud, any contributor can edit directly into the master document from any web browser; the project leader controls the look and feel of the presentation by applying a universal style or theme.

The most-used web-based presentation program today is Google Presentations, part of the Google Docs suite (docs.google.com). This application includes a lot of PowerPoint-like features, and can even import and export files in PowerPoint's format. Other online presentation programs include Preezo (www.preezo.com) and Zoho Show (show.zoho.com).

Presenting on the Road

Here's an added benefit in presenting from the cloud: You can give your presentation anywhere without taking it with you. That's right, you don't have to bother loading a huge PowerPoint file onto your notebook PC's hard disk. Instead, when you get to your destination, connect your notebook to the Internet, open your web-based presentation, and give that presentation in real time to your local audience. In fact, you don't even have to take your notebook with you. You can use any computer at the host location to access and launch your presentation.

Even better, many web-based presentation programs let you give your presentation without even being there! That's right, you can give a remote presentation—at multiple locations at the same time—by having all participants log in to the same web-based spreadsheet. Make sure they have read-only access, dial everyone into a conference call (so that you can provide the audio walkthrough), and then go into presentation mode. All attendees at all locations will see the same presentation, and you don't even have to buy a plane ticket.

Some of these applications include additional features that add functionality to remote presentations. For example, Zoho Show includes integration with Zoho Chat, which lets you have real-time text-based interaction with interested participants. It's like adding a chat room to your presentation; participants ask you questions and you respond, in real time, during the course of the presentation.

Then you have web-based applications such as Cisco's WebEx (www.webex.com) and Microsoft Office Live Meeting (office.microsoft.com/en-us/livemeeting/). These are hosted applications that let you stage live meetings and presentations—called *web conferences*—over the Internet. All group members log onto a designated website and then view the presenter's presentation or participate in real-time audio and video discussions. Granted, a web conference of this sort may be expensive overkill, but it's a very effective way to get the job done—especially if you want live feedback on what you're presenting.

Accessing Documents on the Road

While we're talking about using web-based applications on the road, remember that any application or document housed in the cloud is accessible from wherever you may be. All you need is a computer (and it doesn't even have to be your computer) and Internet access. Log in to the appropriate site, enter your username and password, and then open whatever document you need. It's the same document you worked on back in the office, so you don't have to worry about remembering to synchronize files between computers. Make your changes on the road and you'll see them when you get back to the office. You can even print your documents remotely, if your computer is connected to a printer or you have access to a hotel or conference hall business center.

This is one of the great things about cloud computing; it doesn't matter where you are. You can be in the office, at a trade show, or visiting a client in another city, and you always have access to the same applications and documents. You don't have to worry about taking the right copy of a document with you, or making sure you have a compatible version of the software program loaded on your notebook PC. You always use the same apps, and you always access the same docs. As long as you have a computer and Internet access, it's just like you were in the office.

THE VIRTUAL COMPANY

In the old days, running a business meant renting an office, arranging for a phone line and utilities, hiring a secretary, hiring a staff, and the like. Every morning you left home, commuted to the office, had the secretary handle your phone calls, and managed the staff. Every night you left the office and made the commute back home; you left your work at the office.

Today, however, you often don't have to do any of that. Thanks to the Internet and web-based applications, you can run a one-person company from the comfort of your home. You don't have to spend several hours a week commuting. You don't have to rent expensive office space. You don't have to hire a secretary or a staff. You can do everything yourself, from home, over the Internet.

And, if you decide to take a vacation or a long weekend or just visit the local coffeehouse for a few hours, you can take your office with you. Your notebook computer can access the Internet anywhere there's a Wi-Fi hot spot, and the Internet is where all your applications and data are based. Your customers don't have to know that you're sipping a latte in the corner table at Starbucks or relaxing under an umbrella on the beach; all they know is that you're returning their emails and working on important documents. That you're doing so over the web, using web-based applications, is irrelevant.

The real power of cloud computing is that it lets you run your complete operation by yourself, from anywhere you happen to be. Web-based applications provide all the support you used to get from highly paid employees, and your office itself is in the cloud rather than in an expensive office building. Your costs are lower while your reach is wider. The cloud lets even the smallest business operate like a large enterprise over the web. This truly is the age of the virtual company. Are you taking advantage of all that the cloud has to offer?

Using Cloud Services

Collaborating on Calendars, Schedules, and Task Management

This section of the book takes a look at different types of personal and business computing tasks, and at the web-based applications that can facilitate those tasks. Think of this section as a giant catalog of the best of what cloud computing has to offer: Whatever type of application you're looking for, chances are there's something in the cloud that will do the job for you.

We start our examination of these cloud services with applications that help you get organized—calendars, schedulers, planners, and task management tools. Whether you want to keep a simple group calendar or to-do list or need something more powerful to schedule appointments and meetings, you're sure to find some web-based application in this chapter to your liking.

Exploring Online Calendar Applications

Most computer users today have embraced keeping their schedules on their PCs. Not that the old-fashioned wall-hanging calendar is dead, it's just that it's a whole lot easier to track appointments and events electronically; the computer does all the busywork for you.

The problem, however, with using calendar software (such as Microsoft Outlook or Windows Calendar) is that all your appointments have to reside on a single computer. If you keep a personal calendar on your home PC, you can't reference it from work or when you're traveling. That limits the calculator program's usefulness.

That's why, instead of using a calendar that's wedded to a single computer, many users are moving to web-based calendars. A web-based calendar service stores your calendars on the Internet, where they can be accessed from any computer that has an Internet connection. This lets you check your schedule when you're on the road, even if your assistant in the office or your spouse at home has added new appointments since you left. Web-based calendars are also extremely easy to share with other users in any location, which make them great for collaborative projects.

We'll look at some of the most popular web-based calendars next. Although there are some pay calendars out there, I find the free ones just as functional—and easier for group members to access, since they don't have to pay to use them.

As to favorites, I admit to being a longtime user of Google Calendar; it does everything I need it to do. That said, Yahoo! Calendar does pretty much everything Google Calendar does, and should be another favorite, especially among non-business users. Then there's Apple's new MobileMe Calendar, which is already attracting a lot of attention; it should be considered by anyone also looking at the Google and Yahoo! applications.

Google Calendar

The most popular web-based calendar today, no doubt due to its association with the web's most-used search engine, is Google Calendar (calendar.google.com). Google Calendar is free, full featured, and easy to use. It lets you create both personal and shared calendars, which makes it ideal for tracking business group, family, and community schedules.

> **note** Keep up-to-date with the latest news about online calendar applications with the CalendarReview blog (www.calendarreview.com).

As you can see in Figure 7.1, Google Calendar looks pretty much like every other calendar you've ever seen. You enter your appointments (which Google calls "events") directly into the calendar, which you can display in either daily, weekly, or monthly views. You can also, if you like, view your weekly agenda on a single page.

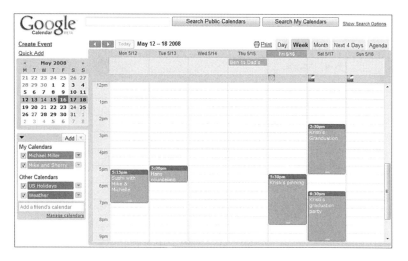

FIGURE 7.1

The easy-to-use interface of Google Calendar. Note the multiple calendars listed in the My Calendars box.

Like all web-based calendars, all your events are stored in the cloud (in this case, the cloud created by Google's own network of servers), not on your own computer. This means that you can access your calendar from any computer anywhere in the world. Just log in to the Google Calendar page and your calendar and all events are there.

Because Google Calendar is web based, you can use it to create not only a private calendar for yourself, but also public calendars for your company or organization. Create a public calendar and all employees or attendees can access it via the web. In addition, special event invitation features make it easy to invite others to an event—public or private.

In addition, Google allows you to create several different—and different types of—calendars. You can create one calendar for home, another for work, and yet another for your son's soccer team. Then you can view all your calendars from the same Google Calendar page, with the events from each calendar color-coded for easy visibility.

What types of calendars can you create with Google Calendar? Here's the list:

- **Personal calendars**, like your default calendar
- **Public calendars**, which others can access via the web
- **Friends' calendars**, which you import from their Google Calendar web pages
- **Holiday calendars**, which add national holidays to a basic calendar

note When you're reading a Gmail message that contains information pertaining to an event, just pull down the More Action menu and select Create Event. This opens a New Event window. Enter the appropriate information, click Save Changes, and the event is added to your Google Calendar.

Setting up a new calendar is comically easy. In fact, there's nothing to set up. When you first sign into the Google Calendar page, your calendar is already there, waiting for your input. There's nothing to create, nothing to configure. Can it get any easier than that?

And here's something unique about Google Calendar. Because it's part of the mighty Google empire, Google Calendar integrates smoothly with Google's Gmail application. Google Calendar can scan your email messages for dates and times and, with a few clicks of your mouse, create events based on the content of your Gmail messages.

For all these reasons, I'm a big fan and longtime user of Google Calendar. I recommend it to any user for home or business use.

Yahoo! Calendar

One of Google Calendar's primary competitors is Yahoo! Calendar (calendar.yahoo.com), hosted by its search competitor Yahoo! This web-based calendar looks, feels, and functions quite similarly to Google Calendar, and is also free for anyone to use.

Yahoo! Calendar's similarity to Google Calendar can be seen in Figure 7.2. To be honest, most web-based calendars have a similar visual look. (How different can you make a calendar look, anyway?) One subtle difference in Yahoo! Calendar, however, is the presence of an Add Task button. This reflects Yahoo! Calendar's offering of tasks in addition to events. You can still add individual items to your daily schedule, but you can also add longer-term tasks and have their due dates show up on your calendar. It's a nice addition.

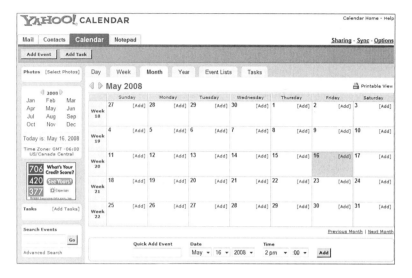

FIGURE 7.2

The familiar look and feel of Yahoo! Calendar.

Of course, you can share your Yahoo! calendars with other users, in a collaborative environment. Just click the Sharing link and indicate how you want to share—no sharing, view-only for friends, view-only for anyone, or view-only with special friends allowed to edit. Choose this last option for true collaboration.

At present, Yahoo! Calendar only lets you create a single calendar. All your events, public and private, have to be stored on this calendar; you can't create different calendars for different functions. (That's one advantage that Google has over Yahoo! here.)

Windows Live Calendar

Because Google and Yahoo! both offer web-based calendars, it's no surprise that the third-largest search site also has a competitive offering. Windows Live Calendar (mail.live.com/mail/calendar.aspx) is Microsoft's web-based calendar, actually part of the Windows Live Hotmail email service.

Windows Live Calendar looks a lot like both of its primary competitors. It offers tasks, like Yahoo! Calendar, and also lets you schedule meetings with other calendar and Hotmail users. (Figure 7.3 shows the page you use to send a meeting request.) Naturally, you can share your calendars with authorized users for group collaboration.

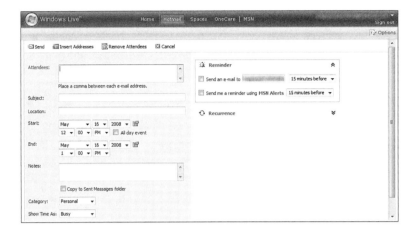

FIGURE 7.3

Scheduling a group meeting with Windows Live Calendar.

Apple MobileMe Calendar

Apple's MobileMe (www.me.com) is a new competitor in the web-based apps market. It includes online mail, contacts, and calendar, as well as an online photo gallery and file storage. We'll examine the other components of MobileMe in the appropriate chapters in this book; for now, let's focus on MobileMe's calendar component.

The MobileMe Calendar is, of course, a web-based calendar that can be accessed from any computer connected to the Internet, Mac or Windows. What makes it more unique and potentially more useful is that it can also be accessed from Apple's iPhone, which makes it a truly mobile calendar. As with competing calendars, you can display MobileMe in daily, weekly, or monthly modes. And, as you can see in Figure 7.4, MobileMe lets you create multiple calendars and display them all on the same screen, using different colors for each calendar. You can also synchronize your MobileMe calendars with Apple's iCal and Microsoft Outlook calendars.

Even though MobileMe Calendar doesn't offer much new or innovative (save for the iPhone interoperability, of course), it's bound to be a strong competitor in the online apps market, especially for non-business users. That's partly because of Apple's cachet (everything Steve Jobs does is cool, for some folks), and partly because Apple does tend to get the details right. Let's face it, MobileMe Calendar looks and feels a little slicker than all its competitors, Google Calendar included. It's certainly worth a look—even if you're already using another online calendar.

FIGURE 7.4

One of the newest web-based calendars—Apple's MobileMe Calendar.

AOL Calendar

America Online isn't quite the powerhouse that it used to be, but it still has millions of users, both paid subscribers and free web users. Any registered user can access AOL Calendar (calendar.aol.com), which integrates with the AOL Instant Messenger (AIM) service for both instant messaging and email. As with competing calendars, AOL Calendar lets you share calendars with authorized users; your calendars can be either private or public.

CalendarHub

Beyond Google, Yahoo!, Apple, and their ilk, many independent sites offer full-featured web-based calendars. Perhaps the most notable of these is CalendarHub (www.calendarhub.com), shown in Figure 7.5.

CalendarHub offers all the features found in the previously discussed web-based calendars—private/public calendars, sharing/collaboration, multiple calendars, task-based to-do lists, and the like. In addition, CalendarHub lets you publish calendars on your blog or website, which makes it great for creating sites for community groups, sports teams, and the like. Other users can sign up to receive email notification of new events, or subscribe to RSS feeds for any calendar view. And, of course, it's completely free.

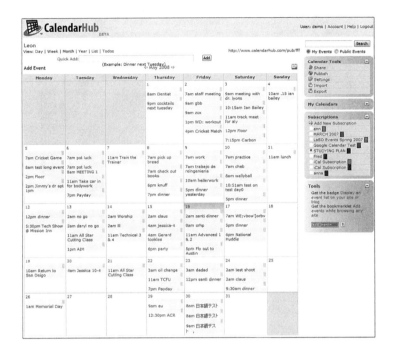

FIGURE 7.5

CalendarHub—one of the most full-featured calendar applications on the web.

Hunt Calendars

Hunt Calendars (www.huntcal.com) offers event-based web calendars. Useful features include email reminders, notification of event conflicts, notification of new and updated events, and the like.

The site lets you add web links and images to calendar events, which is fairly unique. Also nice is the ability to customize the color scheme and graphics to reflect your organization's look and feel, as illustrated in Figure 7.6. This makes Hunt Calendars particularly attractive to businesses and community groups.

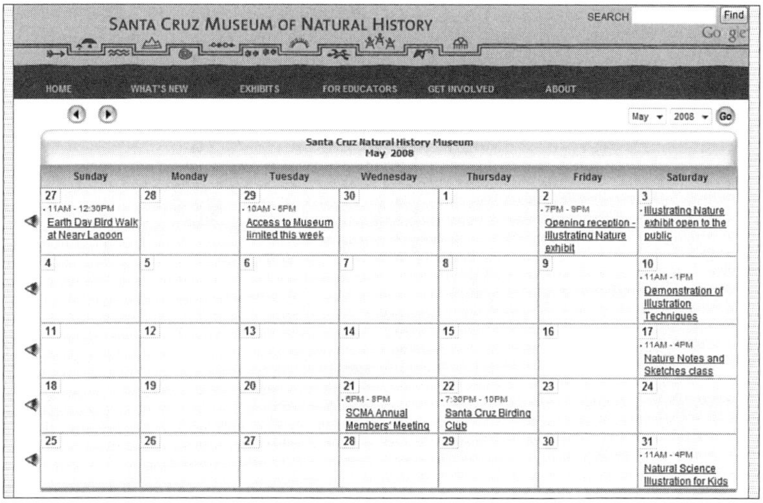

FIGURE 7.6

A customized calendar for the Santa Cruz Museum of Natural History, courtesy of Hunt Calendars.

Famundo

If you keep the schedule for a community group, check out Famundo (www.famundo.com). This site offers Famundo for Organizations, a free web-based calendar ideal for schools, churches, sports teams, and the like. (Figure 7.7 shows a typical school calendar, with different colors used for different types of events.) After the public calendar has been created, users can subscribe to be notified of new and upcoming events. You can also add message boards, blogs, and other features to your calendar.

The company also offers Famundo for Families, a personal version of their Organizations calendar. This version includes a family address book and message board, to facilitate family communication.

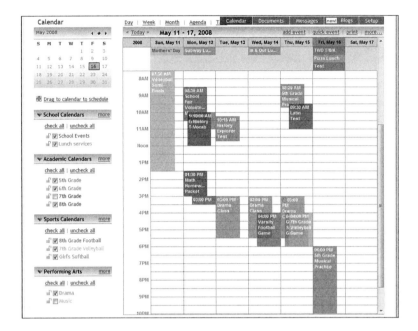

FIGURE 7.7

A school calendar created with Famundo for Organizations.

eStudio Calendar

eStudio Calendar (www.same-page.com/calendar-software.html) is designed specifically for business use. You get three types of calendars in a single interface:

- **Member Event** calendar helps users manage their personal time, keep track of meetings with others, and so on.

- **Team Event** calendar is used to schedule activities for a group, as well as schedule facilities.

- **Supervisor** calendar provides reports to managers about business activities and schedules.

In addition, you can use eStudio Calendar to broadcast information about group activities (via email) and to schedule meetings. Information about company events can also be automatically published to your website.

30Boxes

The name of 30Boxes (www.30boxes.com) refers to the 30 "boxes" displayed on a typical monthly calendar. The site itself offers a slick interface for adding events, as you can see in Figure 7.8. All your events can be shared with other designated users, plus you get to-do lists, a link to Google's Gmail, and similar useful features.

FIGURE 7.8

The easy-to-use interface for entering events into a 30Boxes calendar.

Trumba

Trumba (www.trumba.com) offers web-based calendars ideal for community organizations, schools, and similar public entities. The company lets you embed individualized widgets (dubbed "spuds"), like the one in Figure 7.9, in your own website. These widgets let users view full calendars, add events to the schedule, receive email notification of events, and such.

FIGURE 7.9

A few of the Trumba widgets you can add to your own web page.

Calendars Net

Calendars Net (www.calendars.net) is a free web-based calendar designed for companies or individuals who want to add interactive calendars to their websites. A typical calendar fits into a frame on your website, with little coding required.

The site also hosts personal calendars in the cloud. You can employ four different levels of security (so that different users can view the calendar), add events, edit events, and even change universal calendar settings.

Jotlet

Here's another way to add web-based calendar functionality to your website. Jotlet (www.jotlet.net) is a JavaScript API and library that you can use to build rich calendar functionality into any web page. If you're skilled in HTML programming, this is a good way to build a calendar-based page. The Jotlet API is free for noncommercial use, and also available (for a fee) for commercial sites.

Exploring Online Scheduling Applications

As anyone in a large office knows, scheduling a meeting can be a frustrating experience. Not only do you have to clear time from all the attendees' individual schedules, you also have to make sure that the right-sized meeting room is available at the designated time. Experts claim that it takes seven emails or voice mails to arrange a single meeting; a typical businessperson can spend more than 100 hours each year just scheduling meetings.

Enter, then, the online scheduling application. This web-based app takes much of the pain out of scheduling meetings, for both large and small groups. The typical app requires all users to enter their individual calendars beforehand. When you schedule a meeting, the app checks attendees' schedules for the first available free time for all. The app then generates automated email messages to inform attendees of the meeting request (and the designated time), followed by automatic confirmation emails when attendees accept the invitation.

Professionals who schedule appointments with their clients—doctors, lawyers, hairdressers, and the like—face similar scheduling challenges. For this purpose, separate web-based appointment scheduling applications exist. These apps function similarly to traditional meeting schedulers, but with a focus on customer appointments.

Jiffle

Let's start by looking at web-based solutions for meeting scheduling. Our first app is Jiffle (www.jifflenow.com), which schedules meetings, appointments, and the like for the enterprise environment. To track employees' free time, it synchronizes seamlessly with both Microsoft Outlook and Google Calendar. It also offers its own Jiffle Calendar application.

Jiffle allows the originating user to mark available time slots on his calendar, as shown in Figure 7.10, and then share them with proposed attendees via a Jiffle-generated email invitation. These attendees view the invitation, log in to the Jiffle website, and then select their preferred time slots from the ones proposed. Based on these responses, Jiffle picks the best time for the meeting and notifies all attendees via an automatic confirmation email.

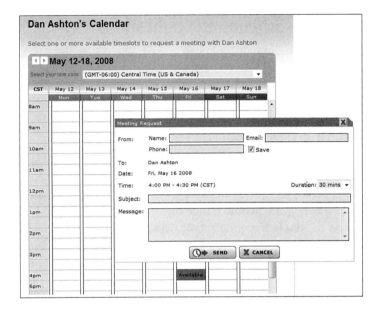

FIGURE 7.10

Scheduling a meeting with Jiffle.

For smaller companies, Jiffle is free for up to 10 meeting confirmations per month. For larger companies, Jiffle Plus, Jiffle Pro, and Jiffle Corporate plans are available.

Presdo

Unlike Jiffle, Presdo (www.presdo.com) is a scheduling tool that isn't limited to a single company. Presdo lets you schedule meetings and events with anyone who has an email address. As you can see in Figure 7.11, adding an event is as simple as entering a description into a box. You then enter the email addresses of other participants, and Presdo emails out the appropriate invites. When an attendee responds, he's automatically added to the event's guest list. (And, for the convenience of all guests, it's a one-button process to add an event to a user's Microsoft Outlook, Google Calendar, Yahoo! Calendar, or Apple iCal calendar.)

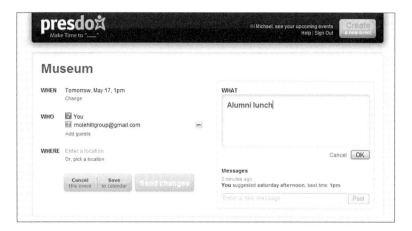

FIGURE 7.11

Viewing a scheduled Presdo event.

Diarised

Diarised (www.diarised.com) is, like Presdo, a web-based meeting maker that users across different companies can use. It helps you pick the best time for a meeting by sending out emails to invitees, letting them choose the best times for them, and then sending you a summary of those best dates. You pick the final date, Diarised notifies everyone via email, and your meeting is scheduled.

Windows Live Events

Event scheduling is now part of Microsoft's bag of tricks. Microsoft's Windows Live Events (home.services.spaces.live.com/events/) is a customized version of its Live Spaces offering; it lets Live Spaces users organize events and share activities between participants.

To schedule an event, you set up a list of invitees and then send out a mass email with a link back to your Live Event site. (All the event details are also available as an RSS feed.) Information about the event is posted on the site itself, which also serves as a place for attendees to come back after the event and share their photos, videos, and blog posts about the event.

With its user-friendly consumer features, Live Events isn't robust enough (or professional enough) for most business users. It is, however, a nice way to plan more personal and informal events.

Schedulebook

Schedulebook (www.schedulebook.com) offers several different types of web-based scheduling services. Depending on the application, you can use Schedulebook to schedule employees, customers, or other interested parties.

The company's three offerings are

- **Schedulebook Professionals**, which is a business-oriented schedule/calendar/planning application
- **Schedulebook Office**, which schedules the use of any shared resource, such as company meeting rooms or even vacation homes
- **Schedulebook Aviation**, which is used by the aviation industry to schedule aircraft, flight training, and similar services

Acuity Scheduling

If you run a business that requires scheduling appointments with clients or customers, Acuity Scheduling (www.acuityscheduling.com) can help ease your scheduling operations. Acuity Scheduling lets you clients schedule their own appointments 24/7 via a web-based interface, like the one in Figure 7.12; you don't have to manually schedule any appointment.

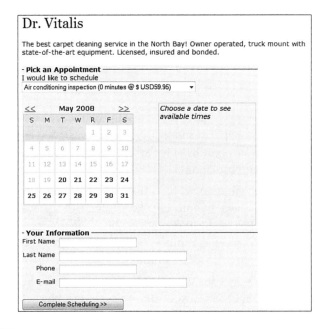

FIGURE 7.12

A typical client scheduling screen from Acuity Scheduling.

You can make the scheduling operation as simple or as complex as you like. For example, some businesses might include new client information forms as part of the online scheduling process. And, of course, the web-based software eliminates scheduling conflict, making for a more efficient schedule for you.

AppointmentQuest

Like Acuity Scheduling, AppointmentQuest (www.appointmentquest.com) is designed to solve the scheduling problems of busy professionals. This application not only enables clients to make and you to accept appointments over the web, it also lets you manage personnel, schedules, and other calendar-related items.

hitAppoint

Our last scheduling application, hitAppoint (www.hitappoint.com), also enables online client booking. Like the previous similar application, it's ideal for any business that requires the making of customer appointments—barbershops, hair salons, doctor and dentist offices, consultants, financial advisors, car repair shops, computer technicians, and the like.

Exploring Online Planning and Task Management

Now let's pivot from schedules to tasks. Planning and task applications let you manage everything from simple to-do lists to complex group tasks, all over the Internet and collaboratively with other users.

iPrioritize

Sharing to-do lists is important for families, community groups, and businesses. Your to-do list might be as simple as a grocery list or as complex as a list of activities for a community program or business project. Whatever the application, iPrioritize (www.iprioritize.com) is a good basic to-do list manager. As you can see in Figure 7.13, authorized users can create a new to-do list, add items to the list, prioritize tasks by dragging them up and down the list, and mark items complete when finished. And, because it's web based, you can access your lists anytime and anyplace.

When you have a list, you can print it out, email it to someone else, subscribe to changes in the list via RSS, and even view lists on your mobile phone—which is a great way to consult your grocery list when at the supermarket!

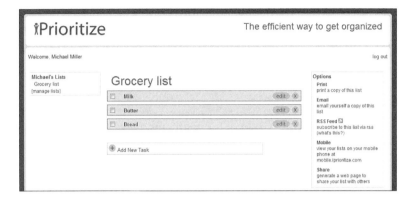

FIGURE 7.13

A simple web-based to-do list from iPrioritize.

Bla-Bla List

Bla-Bla List (www.blablalist.com) is another simple to-do list manager. It's web based, of course, so you can access your lists from any location at any time. You can even publish your lists via RSS so that family and coworkers can get instant updates.

Hiveminder

Hiveminder (www.hiveminder.com) is similar to all the previously discussed to-do list managers. What's nice about Hiveminder is that you can enter list items in a kind of freeform fashion, and it will help you create and prioritize lists based on your "brain dumps."

Remember the Milk

When you need to "remember the milk" at the grocery store, check out the aptly named Remember the Milk (www.rememberthemilk.com) web-based to-do list manager. Once you create a list, you can arrange reminders via email, instant messaging, or text messages to your mobile phone.

Ta-da List

Here's another web-based to-do list manager. Ta-da List (www.tadalist.com) lets you make all sorts of lists, share them with friends, family, and coworkers, and then check off items as they're completed.

Tudu List

Tudu List (www.tudulist.com) is a little different from other to-do list managers in that it also includes a web-based calendar. Items are added both to the appropriate to-do list and to your calendar, on the date they're due.

TaskTHIS

TaskTHIS (taskthis.darthapo.com) is similar to most other to-do list managers, but offers the ability to add extended notes to any individual task. You can publish your tasks via RSS or share with others via the web.

Vitalist

Like other to-do list managers, Vitalist (www.vitalist.com) organizes all sorts of tasks and projects. It's unique in that it uses the Getting Things Done (GTD) workflow methodology popularized by management consultant David Allen.

TracksLife

Trackslife (www.trackslife.com) is a database-oriented task manager. Each "track" is a separate database that combines columns of money, numbers, words, paragraphs, and yes/no responses. The application sends out reminders of critical events via email or RSS.

Voo2Do

Voo2Do (www.voo2do.com) moves beyond simple to-do list management into more sophisticated priority management. This web-based application lets you set up different projects, organize tasks by project, track time spent and remaining on a given task or project, publish task lists, and even add tasks via email.

As you can see in Figure 7.14, Voo2Do tracks pending and completed tasks via a simple dashboard. To view tasks sorted by project, click the Projects tab.

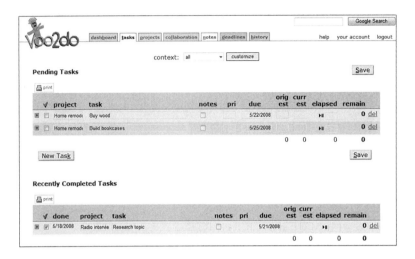

FIGURE 7.14
Viewing tasks and projects with Voo2Do.

HiTask

More sophisticated task management can be had with HiTask (www.hitask.com), a business-oriented task manager. Tasks are added to your calendar and color tagged for easy viewing. The task manager and scheduler both utilize drag-and-drop editing, and you can share and assign tasks and projects to a group of people via the web.

Zoho Planner

Zoho Planner (planner.zoho.com) is perhaps the most sophisticated task planner evaluated here. Its features and functionality approach those of the project management applications we discuss in Chapter 10, "Collaborating on Project Management.

With Zoho Planner, you create a new page for each project you're working on, like the one shown in Figure 7.15. To that project, you add lists with individual to-dos within each list. Each list item can include extensive notes as well as images. You can share each project page with users you designate. Each to-do item also appears on your central calendar.

FIGURE 7.15

Viewing tasks for a particular project in Zoho Planner.

Zoho Planner is ideal for anyone managing small- to medium-sized projects. It's probably overkill for simple to-do list management (try iPrioritize or Remember the Milk, instead), and not powerful enough for large corporate projects. But for the average home or community project, it's an ideal solution—just enough versatility to handle disparate types of projects, but not so complex as to scare off nontechnical users.

PLANNING IN THE CLOUD

Cloud computing offers many advantages when you're trying to keep your life in order. First, of course, you can add and view the things you need to do wherever you are—from any Internet-connected computer and, in many cases, from your handy-dandy cell phone. This is much more useful than it might sound at first blush; always having your to-do list with you is a tremendous productivity boon, possible because of the web-based nature of cloud computing.

Then there's the benefit of collaborating on your task and to-do lists. This may be as simple as you and your spouse putting your heads together for a "honeydew" list, or as complex as managing a large team project. Again, because each user can access the list independently via the web, true collaboration ensues.

Thanks to cloud computing, even a simple to-do list receives all the benefit of "anytime, anywhere" access. You no longer have the excuse of leaving your list at the office or not having input from your spouse; your list is now always with you, and always updated by anyone you authorize to do so.

Does this make you more organized? Yes, if you're the organized type to begin with; these are tools that can enhance your productivity, if you're so inclined. However, if you're not an overly organized person in the first place, all the web-based planning tools in the world won't make you any more so. You have to think and act in an organized fashion before these web-based planning tools can be put into effect. These tools work best for those who use and appreciate them. They don't do much if you don't value organization in your daily life.

Collaborating on Event Management

Scheduling a company meeting is one thing; putting together a large-scale event, such as a conference or seminar or trade show, is quite another. An undertaking of this scale involves more than just clearing a few schedules and making sure the conference room is free at 10 a.m. on Friday. A big event is a big project with lots of individual tasks.

To stage a successful event, you have to market it to potential attendees, sign up those attendees, process their fee payments, make sure that the event space and conference rooms are properly scheduled, handle travel and hotel arrangements, register attendees when they arrive onsite, manage event workers, and make sure everything runs on time during the event. It's a tremendous undertaking.

It's not surprising, therefore, that several companies have introduced web-based event management applications. What's nice about hosting these apps in the cloud is that you can work on the same master database whether you're in your office before the event or sitting at the registration desk during the event. In addition, these web-based apps enable attendees to register in advance online, and for you to process onsite registration via notebook PCs connected to the Internet. Everything you need and use is hosted offsite, on the web, for you to access whenever and wherever you need be.

Understanding Event Management Applications

What exactly does an event management application manage? Less-sophisticated apps may focus on one or two operations, such as event registration or facilities booking. The more full-featured apps include management of everything from pre-event marketing to post-event analysis.

Let's take a look at what you can expect.

Event Planning and Workflow Management

A successful event starts well in advance of its opening date. There are tons of details involved in an event of any size, and managing all those tasks takes quite a bit of computing horsepower—just the thing cloud computing can help you out with. Most event management applications include robust task planning modules, similar to what you'd find in higher-end task management applications or lower-end project management apps.

What you want is the ability not just to track individual tasks in a to-do list fashion, but also benefit from sophisticated workflow management. That is, you need to know which tasks need to be completed before later tasks can be started; you need to know who's doing what, and be alerted to any tasks that are unstaffed or understaffed. In other words, you need the planning and workflow management functionality to continue into the event itself, so that you can manage your staff in an efficient and effective manner.

Event Marketing

Unless you let people know about your event, you could be disappointed with the final attendance. To that end, many event management applications include modules to help you market your event.

For example, many apps offer web-based email marketing, which lets you promote your event via targeted email messages. Other apps help you create your own event website (on their cloud computers), which also helps to promote your event.

Event Calendar

Another part of your event marketing mix is an event calendar—an online calendar that displays all the happenings within your overall event. This proves particularly useful if you're hosting a conference or trade show made of lots of individual panels, sessions, or meetings. You can post each individual event on the main event calendar, easily accessed by any attendee or potential attendee with a web browser.

Facilities Scheduling

Unless you're running a one-room meeting, chances are your event involves multiple rooms and maybe event multiple locations. If so, you need to be able to schedule different rooms for different components of your event; when a participant or group asks for a room, you need to be able to see what's available and when.

To that end, most event management apps include a facilities scheduling module. Ideally, this module ties into the event host's systems, giving you complete power over room or hall scheduling.

Advance Registration

Most larger events require or encourage advance registration of participants. To that end, most event management apps include a web-based registration module, where attendees can sign up (and, in most cases, pay) for the event. Attendee information is entered into a web form, and that data is then stored on the application provider's cloud servers. You then access attendee data from your own computer, wherever you may be.

Some of the more sophisticated advance registration modules provide additional functionality. For example, you might want to collect demographic or other information from attendees, and then use that information to help plan specific programs during the event. Or a registration module might tie into a hotel reservations module, to automatically reserve hotel rooms for those who need them.

The registration module is the backbone of the entire event management program. Make sure it does everything you need it to do, and does so in a way that you find usable.

Payment Processing

Collecting payment for your advance and onsite registrants is a key part of the event management experience. You want the event management software to tie payment processing into the registration process, letting you accept payment via credit card, PayPal, or whatever other payment methods you accept.

Travel Management

If you're running a real "hands-on" event, you might want to consider offering travel services to select attendees. This may be as simple as arranging ground transfer services (taxis, buses, and so on) between your local airport and the event hotel, or as advanced as linking into an online travel site or airline reservations system to provide flight reservations. Although not all event management applications offer this type of functionality, it is available with some apps if you need it.

Housing Management

More common is a housing management module that helps match event attendees with available rooms at your event hotel. Many attendees prefer to have the event host handle their hotel reservations, so that you serve as kind of a "one-stop shop" for all your attendees needs. The best event management apps link directly from advance registration and payment into the hotel's reservation system—and then let you confirm rooms and such at the event site.

Onsite Registration

Your attendees sign up (and probably pay) for your event in advance. But when they arrive on opening day, you need to sign them in, print out badges, provide a welcoming packet, and so forth. All of these tasks are managed by the event management application's onsite registration module. Ideal onsite registration ties into the advance registration and, optionally, the housing management modules of the application. And, because it's all web based, you can manage all onsite activities via a notebook PC at the event site, accessing your main database in the cloud.

Contact Management

Here's a service that many event managers offer attendees. Using the master database of event guests, you can provide contact management services to help attendees get in touch with one another. At the very least, your event management application should let you print out (or host online) a master directory of attendees, which can then be provided as part of the welcoming packet of materials.

Budget Management

Running an event is an expensive and complex undertaking; your overall budget includes hundreds of individual expense items. To that end, your event management application should include a robust accounting or budget management module, to track both your expenses and your income.

Post-Event Reporting and Analysis

When the event is (finally!) over, your job isn't quite done yet. Not only do you have to balance the books, you also need to look back on the entire event and determine how successful it was. That's why most event management applications include some form of post-event reporting and analysis. Some apps even let you send and process attendee surveys, which can provide valuable feedback from those who were there. Look for a reporting module that lets you see at a glance how you performed to plan in a number of areas, not all of them financial. (For example, how many hotel rooms were blocked out in advance versus how many rooms were actually used?)

Exploring Event Management Applications

Now that you know what to look for in an event management application, let's look at the most popular of these web-based apps. Whereas most perform similar functions, some stand out from the pack in terms of what they do—or don't—offer.

123 Signup

Taking these event management applications in alphanumeric order, the first out of the gate is 123 Signup (www.123signup.com). The company offers four different applications: Event Manager, Association Manager, Training Manager, and Member Directory. Of these, the one in which we're interested is the aptly named Event Manager.

note 123Signup claims to be one of the largest event management applications, having processed more than 1,500 events, registered nearly a half million attendees, and handled more than a million individual transactions.

123 Event Manager is scalable, so it can be used for both smaller (employee meetings, stockholder meetings, alumni meetings, and so forth) and larger (trade shows, fundraisers, conferences, and so on) events.

The application handles a combination of front-office and back-office tasks. Front-office tasks include defining and marketing events, automatically generating informational web pages and registration forms, and marketing your event via targeted email messages. Back-office tasks include event registration, badge printing, payment collection, and database management. The program even provides real-time reports on registrations, attendance, collections, and other key factors.

Figure 8.1 shows a typical initial registration page. Potential attendees see information about the event, including a link to a map of the event hotel and the ability to add the event to their Microsoft Outlook calendar. To begin the registration process, an attendee need only click the Register icon; attendees are then prompted for their name and contact info, as well as payment method.

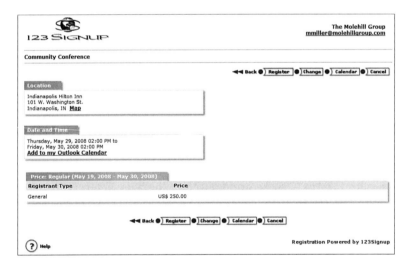

FIGURE 8.1

Beginning the event registration process with 123Signup.

Acteva

Acteva (www.acteva.com) offers online event registration and payments. Using Acteva's web-based solutions, you can handle event registration, ticketing, and payment handling (via any major credit card) directly from your own website. You can then sort and manage all event registration data online.

You start by creating what Acteva calls an Active Page for your event; this is simply a web page with built-in payment handling and data processing. (You create your Active Page by filling in a few web forms—it's quite easy.) After you've published your event page, you then use Acteva's EventMail service to send out notification of your event to potential attendees. Interested parties then visit your Active Page to register and pay for the event. Acteva processes and confirms event registration and sends an email confirmation to the participant. You can then use Acteva's online event management tools to generate will call lists, meal preference lists, name tags, badges, and the like.

Conference.com

Conference.com (www.conference.com) offers one of the most full-featured web-based event management applications available today. By using Conference.com's cloud servers, even small events can utilize the company's powerful event management tools, designed to serve the needs of the largest events. Your data (and the behind-the-scenes application modules) are hosted by Conference.com's secure servers, accessible from any Internet-enabled location.

The company offers a wealth of features for events big and small. You get wizard-based event setup, real-time credit authorization, customizable web pages and forms, onsite processing, and the like. When an event participant submits his registration via your custom-designed web form, the application automatically updates the database on Conference.com's web servers, so your information is always up-to-date.

Conference.com's Event Manager Systems application is actually a suite of interlocking modules, as shown in the diagram in Figure 8.2. These modules include the following:

- **Appointment Manager**, an online meeting scheduling application. This module enables attendees to self-schedule one-to-one sessions with other participants at your event, within time slots that you predefine.
- **Credit Card Manager**, offering real-time credit card authorization integrated into the registration process.
- **Email Manager**, an email broadcasting utility that dynamically pulls recipient names from your registration data.

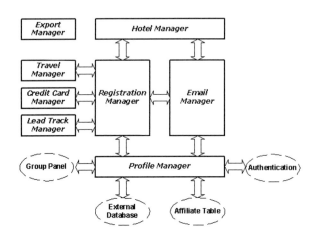

FIGURE 8.2
Conference.com's interlocking event management modules.

- **Export Manager**, an export/import utility that lets you copy the data from one event to another event in your database.

- **Hotel Manager**, a professional room block management tool tightly integrated with the company's Registration Manager module. The system manages everything from small single property blocks to citywide room inventories. Each room type is defined with its own price, description, and starting inventory; as a room is sold, the nightly inventory for that room type is automatically adjusted.

- **Lead Track Manager** uses bar code technology to verify session attendance and provide lead tracking services to exhibitors.

- **Profile Manager** links member, employee, customer, and prospect databases with your conference registration processing, enabling attendees to authenticate themselves through a login web page.

- **Registration Manager** is the core module of Conference.com's Event Manager systems. This module contains the accounting engine, report engine, a graphical report library, and other functions that integrate directly with other modules in the suite.

- **Survey Manager** enables you to create professional-looking online surveys at any point in the event process. You can solicit pre- or post-event attendee surveys; Survey Manager lets you email invitations with hyperlinks that take the user to the correct survey form.

- **Travel Manager**, which helps you manage ground transfer services between multiple airports and event hotels.

Together, this suite of modules creates a full-featured event management application that should handle the needs of any sized event.

Cvent

Competing directly with Conference.com is Cvent (www.cvent.com), with its Event Management system. Like Conference.com, Cvent's Event Management system is a suite of interrelated tools, including the following:

- **Event Registration**, including online event registration, branded event websites, data collection, and generation of name badges and mailing labels

- **Email Marketing**, with automated invitations, "save-the-date" reminders, confirmations, and post-event "thank you" messages

- **Secure Online Payment Processing**, which lets you accept payment by all major credit cards—and offer "early-bird" discounts to motivated participants

- **Housing and Travel Management**, which provides a one-step process for attendees to sign up, pay, get a hotel room, reserve an airline flight, and receive all relevant follow-up communications

- **Contact Management**, which creates a professional directory or address book from all entered participant information

- **Budget Management**, which helps you build, track, and analyze budgets for your events

- **Custom Event Websites**, which helps you launch a custom website for your event—complete with onsite promotion of event sponsors

- **Event Workflow Management**, which helps you manage the entire event planning process from start to finish, complete with to-do list emails for event staff

- **Event Calendar**, a web-based calendar that displays all events open for registration

- **On-Site Functionality**, which enables you to check in attendees as they arrive onsite, provide self-registration kiosks, print session-attendee lists, create bar-coded name badges, and process live credit card payments

- **Event Reporting**, which lets you access event data in real-time via a library of standard and custom reports

Cvent's functionality may be even more than that offered by Conference.com; you should definitely compare the two if you need to manage a large or complex event.

Event Wax

Event Wax (www.eventwax.com) isn't quite as full featured as other event management solutions discussed in this chapter. In fact, it really isn't designed to handle large-scale events such as trade shows and conferences. Instead, Event Wax is for smaller-scale in-house events, such as company meetings, parties, open houses, and the like.

That said, Event Wax performs many of the same functions as the more full-featured programs. You can schedule multiple events, send out email invitations, create event web pages, enable attendee self-registration, and the like. You can even sell tickets for your event, as shown in Figure 8.3, with different types of tickets at different prices.

FIGURE 8.3
Monitoring ticket sales with Event Wax.

eventsbot

Our next event management application is eventsbot (www.eventsbot.com), which offers online event registration and ticketing. You can use eventsbot to plan and manage your event, sell tickets in your choice of currency, collect credit card payments, and even promote your event with major search engines and event directories.

Creating a new event with eventsbot is as easy as filling in a few web forms. This creates a cloud-based website for your event, like the one shown in Figure 8.4. You can then activate ticket selling for the event, which takes place on this web page. After that, eventsbot handles ticket and attendee management for your event.

FIGURE 8.4

A typical eventsbot event page, for the Iota Phi Theta Summer Leadership Conference.

RegOnline

Like eventsbot, RegOnline (www.regonline.com) offers online event registration and payment. You use RegOnline to create a website for your event, create web-based registration forms, accept credit card payments, send automatic email reminders and confirmations, print name badges and room signs, and generate all manner of custom reports. The application also handles the reservations of individual hotel rooms and room blocks.

Figure 8.5 shows how easy it is to get started with RegOnline. This event builder page walks you through the event creation process via a series of web forms. Fill in the relevant information to generate a web page and other functions for your event.

FIGURE 8.5
Using RegOnline's event builder page to create a new event.

Setdot

Setdot (www.setdot.com) isn't really for large corporate events; it's more of a stylish web-based way to schedule and manage smaller personal events and activities. Setdot lets use choose from various preset themes for your event web page. It even displays maps and directions to events. And, although it's mainly for smaller events, it does manage guest responses and messages.

Tendenci

Here's another unique approach to event management. Tendenci (www.tendenci.com) combines a web-based calendar application with online registration and payment. You create an event calendar, like the one in Figure 8.6, which you embed in your own website. When an interested party clicks an event link, he's taken to a dedicated page for that event, where he can see more information and register online. You can then manage the attendee data, print name tags, and the like.

FIGURE 8.6

A typical Tendenci online event calendar, for the Houston chapter of the Public Relations Society of America.

EVENTS IN THE CLOUD

Event management is a process-intensive endeavor. There's so much involved in managing event the smallest event, it really benefits from the power of cloud computing.

Here's the thing: Even a small event has beaucoup number of individual pieces and parts, all of which can benefit from behind-the-scenes computing horsepower. It's seldom cost-effective, however, to purchase the hardware and software to manage these events; you might use the same software applications to manage a 25-person seminar as you do to manage a 1,000-person trade show, even though the 25-person seminar brings in less revenue.

Unfortunately, although both events have the same management needs, the smaller event probably can't afford the traditional type of event management software that the larger event has the budget for.

This is where cloud computing comes to the rescue. By tapping into the same server cloud as the larger event, the smaller event can now afford the same level of event management. The same applications are used, just with less server horsepower.

Cloud computing also lets you take event management from the office to the event site. The attendee database isn't landlocked on your company's computers; it's located on the web, where it's accessible from any web browser. So fire up a series of computer terminals in the event registration room, or just take your notebook PC with you. Everything you or your attendees entered prior to the event is there for your onsite access—which is great not just for onsite registration, but also for solving those niggling problems that always tend to spring up the day of the event!

Collaborating on Contact Management

Most technically adept people today keep their lists of friends, family, and business contacts in some sort of computer-based address book. Maybe it's in the Windows Address Book, maybe it's in Microsoft Outlook, but it's likely that you have all your contacts in some electronic file someplace on your computer.

The problem with that, of course, is what to do when you need to look up an address or phone number and you're not around that particular computer. Maybe you need a phone number for a family member and you're at work, or maybe you need the address for a business colleague and you're at home. You get the idea. Storing your contacts in the cloud would let you access all your contact information from any computer, anywhere.

The situation becomes more acute when your job depends on your contacts, as is the case with salespeople. We're talking customer relationship management (CRM) here, and it's no good to have all your contact information stored on your work computer when you're always on the road. CRM is an ideal application for cloud computing, as witnessed by the large number of firms offering web-based CRM and sales automation applications.

This chapter, then, addresses web-based contact management and CRM solutions. Read on to learn more about storing all your important contact information on the web.

Understanding Contact Management and CRM

Everything we discuss in this chapter is based on the concept of contact management. Whether we're presenting simple address book–based applications or sophisticated sales automation programs, it all comes down to how the application uses the information you provide about a person—which is, in essence, contact management.

All About Contact Management

Contact management is the act of storing information about friends, family, and business colleagues for easy retrieval at a later date. We're talking names, street addresses, email addresses, phone numbers, and the like, stored in some sort of computer file.

Simple computer-based contact management takes the form of an electronic address book, like the Address Book application built in to Microsoft Windows. Applications like Address Book store this contact information on a single computer, where it can easily be recalled and utilized. These programs often interface with your email program, for easy insertion of email addresses.

That said, contact management can be more involved and more useful than simple name/address storage. More sophisticated contact management applications help you track all sorts of details about your friends and colleagues, from personal info (birth date, spouse's name, children's names, favorite restaurants, and the like) to business info (employer, department, job responsibilities, and so forth). These contact management systems typically integrate this personal/professional information with calendar functions and a task manager.

Web-based contact management applications enable you to access your contact information from any computer connected to the Internet. Instead of storing personal contacts on your home PC and work contacts on your office computer, you store all your contacts in the cloud, where they can be accessed from both home and work.

All About CRM

Many businesses require more practical use of their contact information. It's not enough to have the equivalent of a digital Rolodex on hand; that contact information can be injected into various automated processes to help establish and maintain lasting and productive relationships with the company's customers.

This process of managing the needs, wants, and buying patterns of customers is referred to as customer relationship management. CRM helps companies understand and anticipate the needs of current and potential customers; it's an essential tool for building strong customer relationships.

CRM software not only stores customer contact information, it also stores and analyzes all data relating to a particular customer, and then uses that data to help you determine how best to relate with that customer. For example, you can use a CRM program to discover which customers order the most from your company—and then trigger regular phone calls or emails to those customers. Or you can use CRM to find out which customers have the most contact with your technical support department, and then ward off future support calls by proactively sending out support info or scheduling a special support seminar.

When CRM is used by sales staff, you get a subset of CRM called sales force automation, or SFA. SFA applications perform all the customer-centric tasks expected of CRM apps, but with a sales-specific approach. For example, you may use SFA software to track when to make follow-up sales calls or to provide additional information to key prospects.

CRM and SFA applications have been around for decades, almost as long as we've had personal computers. Only recently, however, have these two applications moved into the cloud. As you can imagine, making CRM and SFA web-based makes key contact information (as well as automated processes) available to any salesperson anywhere on the road; all you need to do is log onto the app's website to access important customer data and perform necessary operations.

note Not all CRM applications are as yet fully web based. For example, ACT, one of the most popular CRM software programs, is not a cloud computing application. Although it does offer web access, the application and related data is fully hosted on the company's servers, not in the cloud.

Exploring Contact Management and CRM Applications

The line between contact management, CRM, and SFA applications is blurry enough to make clear distinctions impossible. To that end, we'll look at all three types of applications in one long list—starting with the industry-leading Salesforce.com, and proceeding in alphabetic order from there.

Salesforce.com

The most popular web-based contact management/CRM available today is offered by Salesforce.com (www.salesforce.com). In fact, the company offers several different cloud services:

- **Salesforce.com**, a software-as-a-service CRM application designed for sales, marketing, customer service, and other uses

- **Force.com**, a platform-as-a-service application designed for developers who want to design or customize their own sales force apps

- **AppExchange**, an online marketplace of add-on software for Salesforce.com, developed by independent companies

All these cloud services are buttressed by a robust community and support structure, including blogs, forums, education and training initiatives, and the like.

The company's primary application is the self-named Salesforce.com. The company offers a hosted collection of on-demand business applications that include the following:

- **Sales Force Automation**, which includes activity management, channel and territory management, forecasting, mobile access, email templates, and real-time analytics that help companies increase sales productivity and grow revenues

- **Service & Support**, a customer service solution for enterprise call centers

- **Partners**, a partner relationship management application that enables collaboration and partnership with channel partners

- **Marketing**, which includes tools to execute, manage, and analyze the results of multichannel marketing campaigns

- **Content**, which enables companies to share documents and other content across the organization
- **Ideas**, which helps a company build online communities with their customers, partners, and employees
- **Analytics**, which offers real-time reporting, calculations, and dashboards to help improve decision making and resource allocation

In addition, Salesforce enables clients to build their own custom applications. The company also offers a range of prebuilt industry-specific applications that can be plugged into the main application architecture.

Salesforce offers so many useful applications it's difficult to provide a quick overview, but as an example of the types of applications provided, let's take a quick look at the Activity Management component of the Sales Force Automation module. The specific applications offered in this component include activity tracking and collaboration (to track tasks and activities, schedule joint meetings, and set up automatic templates for recurring tasks), activity scheduling (including the ability to publish calendars for shared resources and set appointment reminders), sales activity reports, and team management functions (assigning and managing a team for large accounts, with specific roles for each team member). All of these tasks help salespeople and sales managers manage complex relationships with demanding customers.

Most Salesforce tasks can be managed via the use of customized dashboards. Each dashboard presents a visual display of key sales metrics. You can create your own custom dashboards to measure those activities of most importance to your company or department. For example, the dashboard shown in Figure 9.1 tracks closed sales to date, sales activity, open support cases, key account performance, leads by source, the top five open leads, and other key metrics.

As you can no doubt gather, Salesforce has applications for companies of any size and type. Pricing is customized for each account, typically costed by number of users and applications used.

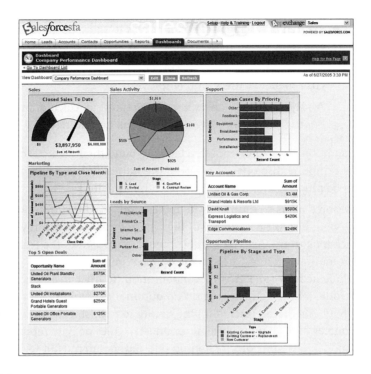

FIGURE 9.1

Tracking key metrics via a custom Salesforce dashboard.

bConnections

As popular as Salesforce.com is, it isn't the only web-based CRM solution available today. Witness bConnections (www.bconnections.com), a contact management program augmented with essential CRM functions for small and medium-sized businesses.

The bConnections application starts with a list of companies you do business with, and a list of contacts at those businesses. (Figure 9.2 shows a typical contact info entry screen.) This contact information is hosted on the web and accessible from any Internet-connected computer.

The application includes a web-based calendar that sales management can use to manage the activities of all their reps. It also tracks leads and sales opportunities, to help you better prepare sales forecasts. All activities are summarized in the application's Executive Summary dashboard.

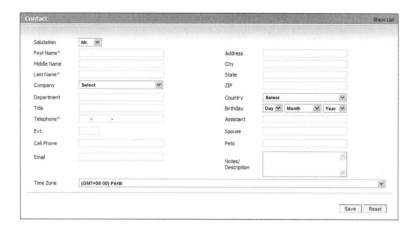

FIGURE 9.2

Entering contact information in bConnections.

BigContacts

BigContacts (www.bigcontacts.com) is a web-based contact manager designed for workgroups as small as 2 people or as large as 2,000. It features an address book, group calendar, task manager, and to-do lists. Its CRM functions include sales tracking, activity reports, team management, and mobile access. Pricing is on a per-user basis.

eStudio Contact Manager

For more basic contact management, check out eStudio Contact Manager (www.same-page.com/contact-management.html). This is application is an online address book specifically designed for business contacts. The address book can be accessed by multiple users from any Internet-connected computer, making it ideal for real-time contact management for sales teams, project groups, and small businesses.

As you can see in Figure 9.3, contacts can be organized into a series of hierarchical folders. Specific contacts can be found by browsing the folders, by browsing alphabetically, or by searching. You can search by any parameter, including name, organization, title, phone number, and the like.

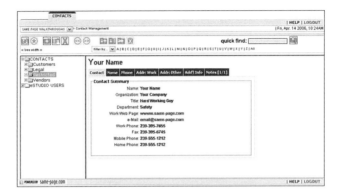

FIGURE 9.3

Viewing the folder-based contact information in eStudio Contact Manager.

Highrise

Highrise (www.highrisehq.com) is a very sophisticated contact management application. Each contact record can include basic info (name, address, email, and so on), as well as notes, file attachments, images, links to audio and video files, emails, and so on. You can even add tasks you need to get done (call, email, send a thank-you note, and so on) regarding this person; these tasks show up in the individual's contact page as well as in your master to-do list.

Contact information (including individual notes and emails) can be aggregated by company on special company pages, like the one shown in Figure 9.4. Key information is summarized on your personal dashboard page, which provides a bird's-eye view of your latest activities and upcoming tasks.

Apple MobileMe Contacts

We discussed MobileMe Calendar in Chapter 7, "Collaborating on Calendars, Schedules, and Task Management." MobileMe Contacts is Apple's new web-based contact management application, useable by anyone with a Mac or Windows computer—as well as anyone using Apple's iPhone, as shown in Figure 9.5.

FIGURE 9.4

Viewing contact data for a specific company with Highrise.

FIGURE 9.5

Apple's MobileMe Contacts, viewed on an iPhone.

MobileMe Contacts (www.me.com) is a straight ahead contact management app with no CRM pretentions. It's essentially an address book stored in Apple's cloud that remains in sync with whatever device you use to access it. It also synchronizes with the contact information in Apple's Address Book and Microsoft's Outlook, Outlook Express, and Windows Contacts programs. Also neat is its integration with Google Maps, which is used to map locations and provide directions.

For millions of iPhone users, MobileMe Contacts will automatically be the contact management application of choice. But here's the thing—it's also a worthy application if you don't have an iPhone; its jazzy interface and synchronization features make it a strong contender for regular PC users, as well.

MyEvents

MyEvents (www.myevents.com) is a combination contact manager, web calendar, task manager, and online community builder. You store all your contacts online, where you can access them via any web browser or wireless device. The calendar function is ideal for both personal and group events, via shared public calendars. Plus you get online file storage and sharing, online digital photo albums, hosted web pages, and community bulletin boards and chat rooms.

Plaxo

Plaxo (www.plaxo.com) is an odd little beast. At its heart, it's an online address book, with contact information stored in the clouds and accessible from any Internet-connected computer. But it's also been accused of being spyware (because its Outlook plug-in is installed automatically when you install various partner software, most notably AOL Instant Messenger).

Plaxo's status as cloud service comes from the hosting of contact information on the company's servers, and the automatic sending of invitations to all contacts in a user's email address book. When information on a specific contact is updated by one user, that updated contact information automatically appears in the address book of all other users who have that person as a contact. (Figure 9.6 shows a typical Plaxo contact page.)

More recently, Plaxo has altered its offerings to include more social networking types of functionality, as well as a web-based calendar. The company was also acquired by Comcast, which intends to use Plaxo to drive its SmartZone communications hub.

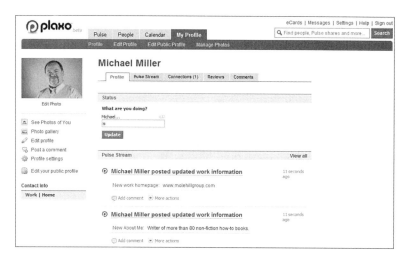

FIGURE 9.6

A typical Plaxo contact profile.

People Matrix

People Matrix (www.wolfereiter.com/PeopleMatrix.aspx) is a web-based contact management application tweaked for human resources use. In addition to basic contact management, it includes job applicant data, and lets users send mass emailings about job postings and the like. You can also use the program to post job announcements to your company's existing website, accept online job applications, and track your history of communications with individual contacts.

PipelineDeals

PipelineDeals (www.pipelinedeals.com) offers an easy-to-use web-based CRM solution. The application lets you track contacts, leads, milestones, deal status, and other key data. As the name implies, PipelineDeals is deal focused. You attach all data and accompanying files (Word documents, Excel spreadsheets, and so on) to a specific page for each current or pending deal.

One of the key reporting features in PipelineDeals is the Deal Home Page, a dashboard that provides a quick snapshot of deal status and upcoming activities. Events and activities also display on the program's integrated web calendar.

SalesBoom

SalesBoom (www.salesboom.com) provides web-based CRM and back-office solutions, with different editions for different-sized businesses:

- **Enterprise Edition**, for larger organizations. Includes inventory management, product management, accounting, and human resources management solutions.
- **Professional Edition**, for medium-sized businesses. Includes marketing automation, sales force automation, and customer service and support solutions.
- **Team Edition**, for small businesses. Includes sales force automation, contact management, and customer service and support solutions.

All of SalesBoom's sales force automation solutions include lead management, contact management, account management, opportunity management, and forecasting features. The Enterprise Edition also includes quote management, contract management, commissions management, and a product database.

SalesJunction.com

SalesJunction.com (www.salesjunction.com) offers a web-based CRM and SFA contact management system, priced on a per-user basis. Unique features include management of service cases, mass email sales campaigns, and sales pipelines. (Figure 9.7 shows a Sales Funnel report, which provides a breakdown of activity in an individual sales pipeline.)

The company's Pro Edition also includes territory management functionality, which lets companies set up, assign, and work leads by territories. Individual users can be assigned to multiple territories, and managers can be assigned to manage as many territories as you like.

SalesNexus

Web-based contact management software is what SalesNexus (www.salesnexus.com) offers. It was designed from the ground up around the needs of salespeople, sales management, and marketing professionals.

SalesNexus features include the ability to create and store proposals, estimates, quotes, and sales sheets; customized sales pipeline and activity reporting; management of automated email marketing campaigns; and automatic lead creation from website forms. In addition, SalesNexus can capture and report the source of website leads.

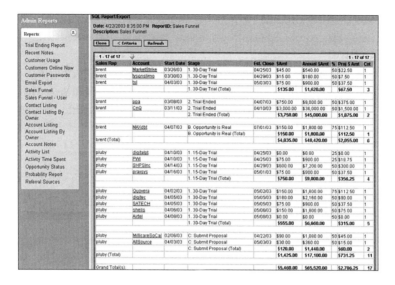

FIGURE 9.7
Tracking sales pipeline activity via a SalesJunction.com Sales Funnel report.

The SalesNexus contact database cleanly interfaces with your company's email system, so that all inbound and outgoing emails between a contact and anyone in your organization are automatically attached to the contact's record. The application also includes support for mobile phone and handheld digital devices, and syncs with Microsoft Outlook contacts, calendars, and tasks.

Zoho CRM

Our final contact management/CRM application is Zoho CRM, available in three different editions: Free Edition (for up to three users), Professional Edition, and Enterprise Edition. The application includes the following modules:

- **Sales & Marketing**, which integrates sales with campaigns, leads, sales pipeline, and forecasts
- **Inventory Management**, which provides a complete integrated inventory management system
- **Customer Support & Service**, which employs cases and solutions to integrate the customer support process with sales data
- **Reports & Dashboards**, which help you analyze sales and marketing trends and key metrics

The application also includes an Outlook plug-in that enables you to synchronize your Zoho CRM contacts, tasks, calendar, and emails with Microsoft Outlook.

Zoho's Sales & Marketing component is a full-fledged CRM/SFA application. It includes lead management, opportunity management, account management, contact management, activity management, sales management, and sales quotas functions. For example, Figure 9.8 shows Zoho CRM's Potentials tab, which tracks sales opportunities end to end in the sales cycle.

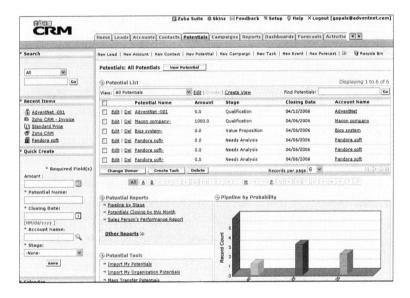

FIGURE 9.8

Tracking sales opportunities in Zoho CRM's Potentials tab.

CRM: MORE THAN JUST SOFTWARE

Customer relationship management may have started out as a software application championed by ACT, SAP, and other technology companies, but it has grown into a holistic business philosophy. The goal of CRM is to solidify customer relationships, and in turn increase profits by reducing the costs associated with selling to each customer. Although some of this can be accomplished via software (both traditional and cloud based), it takes a lot more than technology to fully achieve the goal.

The key to making CRM work is to adopt a customer-centric approach. Technology is just one part of a three-pronged initiative; a company must also include its people and processes in its CRM strategy.

All the people throughout the company—from the CEO to each customer service rep—must embrace the customer-centric approach. The company's processes must then be changed to support the CRM initiative; the company must also ask how this process can better serve the customer. Finally, the company must select the best technology to drive these improved processes, typically in the form of cloud-based CRM solutions.

Building customer relationships doesn't happen by just subscribing to a web-based CRM application. For CRM to be truly effective, the entire company must buy into the initiative. Yes, cloud computing can help, but it's just a part of the solution. For CRM to truly take hold, the company must be serious about changing to a customer-based focus.

Collaborating on Project Management

Managing a large project can be an exhaustive task. Even the smallest project has numerous pieces and parts, all of which have to be completed in a precise order and on an exacting timetable for the project to come in on time and on budget. If just one piece slips, the whole project goes out of whack.

The process of managing a project gets even more complex when the participants are in different locations. How do you keep track of the tasks that need to be completed by someone in your Denver branch when you're in New York? Or what about components that must be completed by outside vendors? It's a real nightmare.

Although you can't always turn a nightmare into a dream project, cloud computing can help alleviate the night sweats associated with this sort of complex project management. When you employ a web-based project management application, you can more easily manage all the pieces and parts, no matter where the players are located. Your project is turned into a single database hosted in the cloud, accessible by all from any Internet-connected computer.

Understanding Project Management

Put simply, project management is the act of planning, organizing, and managing resources to bring about the successful completion of specific project objectives. The project itself can be anything, from creating a product brochure to implementing a new hiring process to launching a new product line. What all projects have in common, however, is that they're finite endeavors—every project has a specific start and completion date. And it's to this latter date that you must manage.

The challenge, of course, is completing the project by the assigned date—and to the agreed-upon budget. Key to this is the tight management of each and task that comprises the project; if all the component tasks are completed on time and on budget, the entire project will be completed as planned. If one or more tasks slip—and you can't make up the lost time elsewhere—your project will come in late.

To manage the individual tasks within a project requires managing a larger set of resources—people, of course, but also money, materials, space, communications, and the like. This resource management is crucial to ensuring the eventual success of a project.

Project management professionals like to think in terms of juggling a certain set of constraints: scope (what must be done to produce the end result), time (the amount of time available to complete the project), and cost (the budgeted amount available for the project). These constraints are interrelated; one constraint can't be changed without impacting the others. For example, if you increase the scope of a project, you typically need to increase the time and cost, too. If you want to reduce the time to complete the project, you might need to increase the costs (pay more to get it done faster) or reduce the scope (try to accomplish less things on a tighter schedule).

The key to effective project management is to use all available tools and techniques that enable the project team to organize their work to meet these constraints. And, not surprisingly, one such tool is a web-based project management application.

note These three constraints (scope, time, and cost) are often referred to as the project management triangle, with each side of the triangle representing a constraint.

Exploring Project Management Applications

Traditional project management software helps project managers and team members organize and track all the various tasks in a project. To do this, the software typically includes scheduling, budget management, and resource-allocation components. Web-based project management applications do all this online, with a centralized project file accessible to all team members. This enables improved communication and collaboration between members of the project team.

> **note** Some of the best-selling traditional desktop projection management programs include Microsoft Project, Primavera Project Planner, and FastTrack Schedule.

The scheduling component of a project management application helps the project manager schedule the series of events that comprise the total project. This should include a list of dependencies—those events that need to be completed before other events can start. The project management application should then be able to calculate the project's critical path, which is the series of events that determine the length of the entire project.

After the project has been planned, it then has to be executed. The project management application should enable this execution by creating task lists for team members, allocation schedules for project resources, overview information for the team manager, and, as the project progresses, an early warning of any risks to the project's completion.

All that said, most web-based project management applications work in a similar fashion. Let's examine some of the most popular of these cloud services.

@task

The web-based project management program known as @task (www.attask.com) offers a variety of traditional projection management functions. The application includes an interactive drag-and-drop Gantt chart (shown in Figure 10.1), critical path analysis, project milestones, planned/projected/estimated comparisons, resource scheduling, issue management, and calendar views for project tasks. Tasks can even be managed remotely via a special software widget for Apple's iPhone.

> **note** A Gantt chart is a type of bar chart that illustrates a project schedule. Individual tasks appear as discrete bars on the chart. Dependent tasks are linked to the end of prior activities.

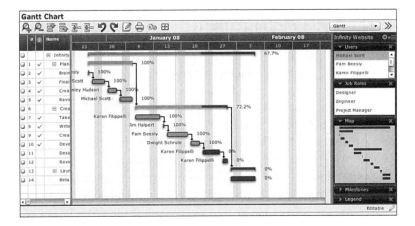

FIGURE 10.1
The drag-and-drop Gantt chart in @task.

AceProject

AceProject (www.aceproject.com) is an easy-to-use web-based project management application. It lets users manage multiple projects using multiple resources and share those resources across projects. Tasks can be tracked via a variety of filters that fine-tune the results, and the application offers a number of different project reports and statistics. AceProject also offers time tracking, email notification of task deadlines, and a monthly project calendar, shown in Figure 10.2. The start and end dates are shown on their individual dates (in green and red, respectively).

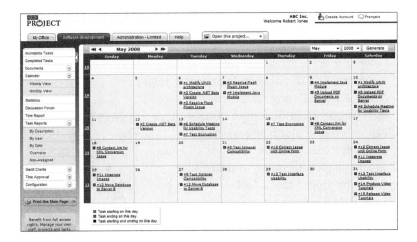

FIGURE 10.2
AceProject's web-based project calendar.

Basecamp

One of the most popular project management applications today is Basecamp (www.basecamphq.com). Its web-based nature makes it viable for both internal and external (client) projects.

Project management is provided via a special dashboard, shown in Figure 10.3. The dashboard displays all projects and clients on a single screen, with late items and those due soon highlighted on the screen.

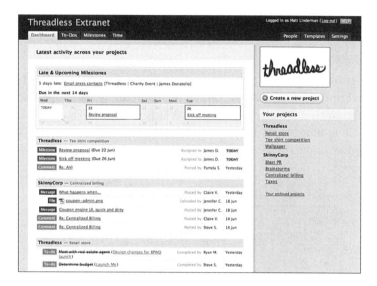

FIGURE 10.3

Basecamp's project management dashboard.

In addition to standard project management operations such as time tracking and milestones, Basecamp includes to-do lists, file sharing, message boards, wiki-like web-based documents, and other group collaboration features. All web-based pages created by the program can be fully customized.

One of the aspects of Basecamp that makes it so appealing is its price. The company offers three different plans (Basic, Plus, and Max), priced from a flat $24/month to $149/month. This is in contrast to similar applications that price on a per-user basis. Basecamp's flat pricing makes it easy for organizations of any size to pick the plan that's right for them, based on the number of concurrent projects and storage space needed.

Copper Project

Copper Project (www.copperproject.com) is a project management application that can be hosted either on the company's servers or on your own server. Either version enables web-based collaboration.

Copper includes useful features such as a drag-and-drop weekly or monthly timeline, resource management, email alerts, statistical reports, and a unique personal time management tool. The program's Springboard view lets you see the progress of multiple projects on a single screen; you can drill down from there by client or project.

eStudio TaskTracker

TaskTracker from eStudio (www.same-page.com/online-project-management-07.html) is an easy-to-use online project management application. This program includes features such as task lists (shown in Figure 10.4), work logs, issue management, automatic task dependencies, subproject capability, budget and expense tracking, Gantt charts, and a full set of management reports.

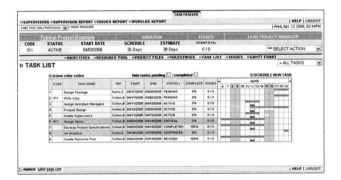

FIGURE 10.4
An eStudio TaskTracker task list.

onProject

Another company offering online projection management solutions is onProject (www.onproject.com). The company's myonProject application is a subscription service that offers collaborative project management functionality. The application's Workspace page provides one-screen access to all key operations. Other useful features include Gantt charts, time and expense tracking, issue tracking, a web-based task calendar, automatic email notifications, file sharing, group discussion forums, contact management, and full project reporting. Pricing is on a per-user basis.

Project Drive

The Project Drive (www.project-drive.net) application includes communication and collaboration features in addition to basic project management functionality. Users get a customizable overview dashboard, templates for fast project setup, Gantt charts, task management, resource allocation, document sharing and management, automated communication tools, a group calendar, cost analysis and budgeting, and a large number of management reports.

Vertabase

Vertabase (www.vertabase.com) is a popular web-based project management application. It offers a summary executive dashboard, multiple schedule views, project portfolio, cross-project Gantt charts, resource planning, budget control, issue tracking, and a detailed project schedule.

Wrike

Wrike (www.wrike.com) is a project management application that offers a unique way to create project tasks. The application is email based; emails from project members are automatically converted into tasks in the appropriate project. Wrike then automatically reminds employees about overdue tasks, creates individual schedules for employees, and generates Gantt charts for each project.

Zoho Projects

Our final web-based project management application is Zoho Projects (projects.zoho.com), another popular product from the Zoho cloud combine. Zoho Projects is a standard project management application, complete with tasks and milestones, a project calendar, Gantt charts and other reports (including the task list view shown in Figure 10.5), time tracking, and group file sharing.

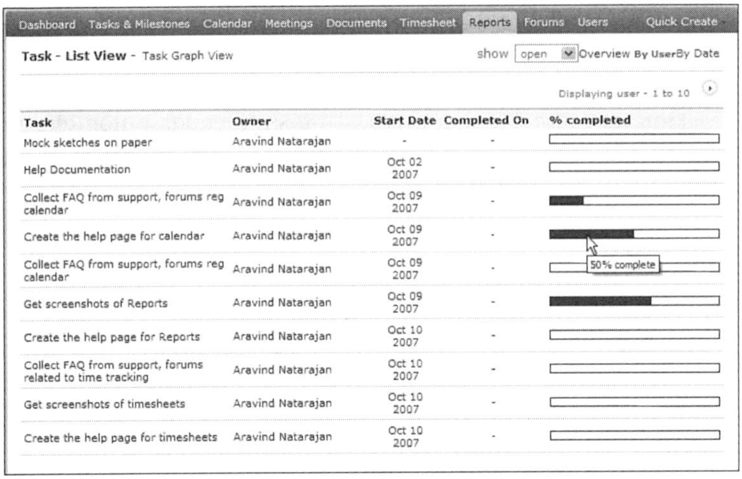

FIGURE 10.5

View project tasks in list view with Zoho Projects.

Zoho offers several different versions of the Projects application, from a single-project Free version to the Enterprise version that lets you manage an unlimited number of projects. Pricing ranges from free to a flat $80 per month.

THE ADVANTAGES OF MANAGING PROJECTS ONLINE

The advantages of using project management software are well known; when you have a large number of resources and constraints to juggle, it makes sense to let technology do a lot of the detail work for you. But there are even more advantages to using a web-based project management application, especially if your projects involve participants and resources that aren't all based out of the same location.

Naturally, a web-based application lets participants from different locations access the same master project files. When the master project is housed in the cloud, there are no issues with maintaining the right versions of files for all users, or with synchronizing files among computers to make sure they're all up-to-date. Users can access files from any Internet-connected computer using any web browser.

Of course, cloud project management services also let smaller companies tap into more powerful applications. A small company pays only for the resources used, and can easily scale upward if a single project grows in size or if the company needs to manage additional projects. That one-time cost of traditional software is turned into a pay-as-you-go charge.

In addition, using web-based services facilitate improved communication between team members. Many web-based project management applications include email, blogs, message boards, and chat rooms for use by project members. When everything takes place on the web, it's a lot easier for team members to talk to each other.

This, in turn, facilitates group collaboration—which is what large projects are all about. The more efficiently and effectively you collaborate, the fewer glitches you'll encounter over the course of the project. And that's a very good thing.

Collaborating on Word Processing

Just about everyone who uses a computer uses a word processing program. You use your word processor—most likely some version of Microsoft Word—to write memos, letters, thank you notes, fax coversheets, reports, newsletters, you name it. The word processor is an essential part of our computing lives.

But what do you do when you don't have your word processor at hand? Maybe you're visiting your parents' home for the holidays and you want to catch up on your memo writing, but your folks don't have a computer in the house—or they do, but it doesn't have Word installed. Or maybe you're on a short business trip, without your trusty notebook PC, and you need to fire off a short letter for work. Or perhaps you're a student on campus with an assignment due, and you left your computer back in the dorm.

In short, what do you do when you don't have Microsoft Word handy? The solution, believe it or not, lies in the clouds—in the form of a web-based word processor.

That's right, there are a number of web-based replacements for Microsoft's venerable Word program. All of these programs let you write your letters and memos and reports from any computer, no installed software necessary, as long as that computer has a connection to the Internet. And every document you create is housed on the web, so you don't have to worry about taking your work with you. It's cloud computing at its most useful, and it's here today.

How Web-Based Word Processing Works

Microsoft Word is a software program that is installed on your computer's hard disk. Web-based word processors, in contrast, are hosted in the cloud, not on your hard drive—as are the documents you create with these applications. And these web-based applications mimic the key features of Microsoft Word, so you don't give up much in the way of functionality. Read on to learn more.

Benefits of Web-Based Word Processors

As you're by now well aware, the most obvious benefit of using a cloud service is that your documents can be accessed wherever you are, from any PC. With a web-based word processing application, you'll never discover that the document you need is located on your office PC when you're at home or away.

Also nice is that, by being web based, you can easily share your documents with others. That makes real-time workgroup collaboration possible from anywhere around the globe, which is something you don't have with Microsoft Word and similar desktop software programs.

Another benefit of being web based is that you can't lose your work—theoretically, anyway. After you've named the document you're working on, the web-based word processor saves your file on its cloud of servers. From that point on, every change you make to the document gets saved to the cloud servers automatically. Nothing gets lost if you close your web browser, navigate to another website, or even turn off your computer. Everything you do is saved on the web.

Best of all, most of these web-based applications are free. That's free, as in it costs zero dollars, unlike the ever increasingly expensive Microsoft Office suite.

Being free makes it easy to take for a test drive, and even easier to add to your bag of applications. Many early users who've tried these web-based applications have said that they're likely to switch from Microsoft Word. These cloud services can perform nearly all of Word's basic functions, which makes them perfect for corporate and small business environments.

Should You Use a Web-Based Word Processor?

Before you jump into the web-based word processing waters, you need to ask whether a cloud service is right for your particular needs. The answer, of course, is that it all depends.

Here are the following users for whom web-based word processing holds promise:

- **Beginning users.** If you're just starting out in the word processing world, there's no better place to start than with a web-based application. The slightly limited functionality of these cloud apps actually works to the benefit of beginning users. You won't be overwhelmed by all the advanced options that clutter the Microsoft Word menus. Plus, most of these web-based word processors are extremely easy to use; everything you need is right out in the open, not hidden inside layers of menus and dialog boxes. I'll be honest with you—I wish I'd had a word processor like Google Docs 20 years ago, when I was learning how to use PC-based word processing programs.

- **Casual users.** A web-based word processor is also a good choice if you have modest word processing needs. If all you're doing is writing memos and letters, a web-based application gets the job done with ease.

- **Anyone who wants access to their documents from multiple locations.** If you work on the same data at work and at home (or on the road), you know what a hassle it is to carry your data around with you from computer to computer—and keep it synchronized. A web-based word processor solves this problem. Wherever you are (home, office, on the road), you're always accessing the same version of your document, stored in the cloud. There are no synchronization issues; you work on the same file wherever you go.

- **Anyone who needs to share their documents with others.** Sometimes you need others to view what you're working on. Maybe you have a family budget that you and your spouse both need to see. Maybe you have a soccer team schedule that other parents need to view. Whatever the need, a web-based word processor lets you share your documents with anyone you like, over the Internet.

- **Anyone who needs to edit their documents in a collaborative environment.** Sharing is one thing; collaborative editing is another. If you need multiple users to both access and edit data in a document, a web-based word processor lets you do things that are impossible in Microsoft Word. For example, I know of one entrepreneur who adopted Google Docs for his small telemarketing company. He has five employees making calls at the same time, all from their homes. He has all five employees work from the same document; they not only access the same call data, they also enter their results into the document—live, via the Internet.

All that said, a web-based word processor isn't for everyone. So who *shouldn't* use one of these applications?

- **Power users**. If you've created your own custom documents or templates in Microsoft Word, especially those with fancy macros and the like, a web-based word processor is not for you. Most of these cloud applications lack Word's most advanced features and just won't get the job done.

- **Anyone who wants to create sophisticated printouts**. Most of today's web-based word processors lack some of the more sophisticated formatting options that some Word users take for granted. With a word-based word processor, what you see onscreen is exactly what prints out—for better or for worse. If you need fancy printouts, a web-based application will probably disappoint.

- **Anyone working on sensitive documents**. Web-based applications (and documents stored on the web) are not good tools if your company has a lot of trade secrets it wants to protect. In fact, some organizations may bar their employees from working on documents that don't reside on their own secured servers, which rules out a web-based word processor entirely.

- **Anyone who needs to work when not connected to the Internet**. This is the blatantly obvious one, but if you're not connected to the Internet, you can't connect to and work with a web-based application. To work offline, you need Microsoft Word.

So, if you're a beginning or casual user who doesn't need fancy printouts, or if you need to share your documents or collaborate online with other users, a web-based word processor is worth checking out.

Exploring Web-Based Word Processors

There are a half-dozen or so really good web-based word processing applications, led by the ever-popular Google Docs. We'll start our look at these applications with Google's application and work through the rest in alphabetic order.

Google Docs

Google Docs (docs.google.com) is the most popular web-based word processor available today. Docs is actually a suite of applications that also includes Google Spreadsheets and Google Presentations; the Docs part of the Docs suite is the actual word processing application.

note Google Docs is based on the Writely web-based word processor, originally developed by the software company Upstartle. Google acquired Upstartle in March 2006, and subsequently mated it with its home-grown Google Spreadsheets application.

Like all things Google, the Google Docs interface is clean and, most important, it works well without imposing a steep learning curve. Basic formatting is easy enough to do, storage space for your documents is generous, and sharing/collaboration version control is a snap to do.

When you log in to Google Docs with your Google account, you see the page shown in Figure 11.1. This is the home page for all the Docs applications (word processing, spreadsheets, and presentations); all your previously created documents are listed on this page.

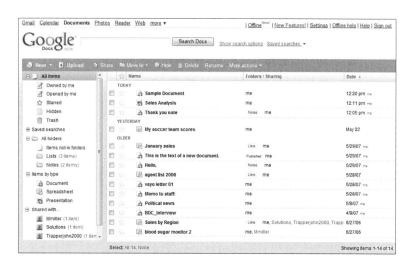

FIGURE 11.1

The Google Docs home page—where all your documents are listed.

The leftmost pane helps you organize your documents. You can store files in folders, view documents by type (word processing document or spreadsheet), and display documents shared with specific people.

The documents for the selected folder or filter are displayed in the main part of the window. As you can see, word processing documents are noted with a document icon, spreadsheets have a spreadsheet icon, and presentations have a presentation icon. To open any document, click the item's title. The document will open in a new window. To delete an item, select it and then click the Delete button.

To create a new word processing document, click the New button and select Document. The new document opens in a new browser window, as shown in Figure 11.2. Your document looks like a big blank space in this new browser window, one with a pull-down menu and toolbar at the top. You use the toolbar buttons and the functions on the pull-down menu to edit and format your document.

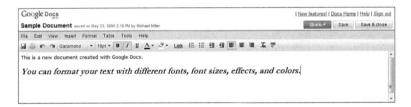

FIGURE 11.2

A new Google Docs document.

As with all web-based word processors, when you create a Google Docs document, you're actually creating an HTML document—just like a web page. All HTML-type formatting is available for your documents, through the Google Docs interface. The document is also saved in HTML format, although you can export (download) the document in a number of other formats, including Microsoft Word DOC format and Adobe PDF.

Of course, one of the most useful features of Google Docs is the capability to share a document with other Google Docs users, either for viewing or for collaborative editing. To share a document or spreadsheet for viewing or collaboration, click the Share button and select Share with others. This displays the Share This Document page, shown in Figure 11.3.

note You can also use Google Docs to work on files you've previously created in your regular word processing program—including Microsoft Word. Just click the Upload button to display the Upload a File page. Browse for the file you want to upload, and then click the Upload File button.

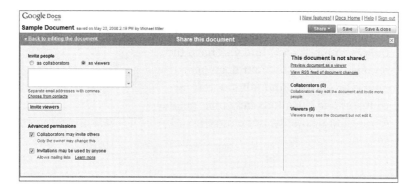

FIGURE 11.3

Getting ready to share a Google Docs document.

In the Invite People box, enter the email addresses of the people you want to share the document (separate multiple addresses with commas). If you want others to just view the document without being able to edit it, check the As Viewers option. If you want others to be able to edit the document, check the As Collaborators option. Click the Invite Viewers or Invite Collaborators button to send out the invitations.

Your recipients now receive an invitation via email. The invitation contains a link to the document; clicking this link opens the document in a new browser window. Invited viewers can navigate around the entire file and also save that file to their personal Google Docs online storage area or as a file to their own PC. Anyone invited as a collaborator can edit the file, in real time; in fact, multiple users can edit the document at the same time. It's like each of you is sitting next to each other, all typing away at the same keyboard at the same time.

Finally, there's a relatively new feature in Google Docs that some users might find beneficial: the ability to work on your documents offline, without an Internet connection. To use Google Docs Offline, as this feature is called, click the Offline link to download and install Google Gears, a software tool that converts Google online apps into traditional desktop apps. While this defeats some of the aspects of cloud computing, it does let you work on your documents literally anywhere—even when there's no Internet connection to be found.

caution When you work on Google documents offline, you lose some of the app's native formatting—most importantly, the revision marks that are so useful when you're collaborating on a group document.

Bottom line, Google Docs is a good full-featured web-based word processor. Collaboration is easy, and you have the option of working on your documents offline if you like. And, although some competing applications may offer greater

note Buzzword was originally developed by a company named Virtual Ubiquity, and acquired by Adobe in September of 2007.

formatting flexibility, none have near the installed base of users that Google Docs has.

Adobe Buzzword

Buzzword (buzzword.acrobat.com) is Adobe's entry into the web-based word processor marketplace. Unlike Google Docs, Buzzword runs in Flash, which might be problematic for users with older PCs or those with slow Internet connections. That said, Flash implementation gives Buzzword a snazzy interface and some advanced editing and formatting features.

As you can see in Figure 11.4, the Buzzword interface is head and shoulders above the more utilitarian interface of Google Docs. In addition, Buzzword gives you full text and paragraph formatting, headers and footers, page numbering, endnotes, and keyboard shortcuts, none of which are currently available with Google Docs. You also get a running word count, inline spell checking as you type, the ability to insert comments, and a history of revisions made to a file. Those features make Buzzword a great tool for professional writers.

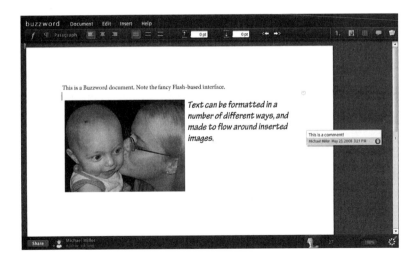

FIGURE 11.4

Adobe Buzzword's elegant Flash-based interface.

Buzzword is also versatile when it comes to working with images. You can import JPG, GIF, and PNG files into any Buzzword document, and then size and place those images as you like. Buzzword flows text around the imported images even better than Word does.

When collaborating with other users, you get granular control over whether contributors can share (Reader level), make comments (Reviewer), or write to (Co-Author) a document. The commenting structure for collaborating is particularly nice; all you have to do is highlight a piece of text and then stick a virtual note in the margin.

ajaxWrite

Unlike most other web-based word processors, ajaxWrite (www.ajaxwrite.com) doesn't work with Internet Explorer. Instead, you have to use the Firefox web browser. This not unimportant caveat aside, ajaxWrite's simple interface and clean workspace makes it well liked by many users.

As you can see in Figure 11.5, ajaxWrite looks a lot like Microsoft Word, which makes it easy to start using the program right away. New documents open in their own windows, complete with Word-like pull-down menus and toolbars. It's a familiar experience, even if it doesn't include all the paragraph and document formatting features you get with Word (or with Adobe Buzzword, for that matter).

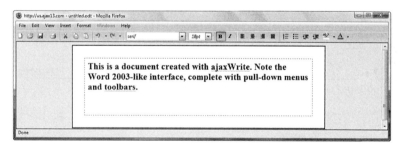

FIGURE 11.5

The Word-like interface of ajaxWrite.

And here's something else you don't get with ajaxWrite: group collaboration. Unlike the other web-based word processors discussed in this chapter, ajaxWrite offers no sharing or collaboration features. It's purely a single-user application.

Docly

Docly (www.docly.com) is an interesting application, designed especially for professional writers. What sets Docly apart from other web-based word processors is its focus on copyright management, including the ability to assign a document a Creative Commons license or a traditional "all rights reserved" license. This means that not only can you share and publish your Docly documents, you can also offer them for sale.

note Creative Commons is a not-for-profit organization that has released several different copyright licenses that regular people can use to restrict how others use their work. Learn more at www.creativecommons.org.

As you can see in Figure 11.6, Docly offers a minimalist approach to editing and formatting. The editing window itself is rather small, in part to make room for a bewildering number of formatting buttons in a toolbar on top. It's not the most elegant interface, but it gets the basic job done.

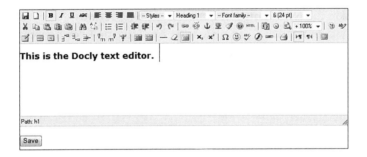

FIGURE 11.6
Docly's small and confusing text-editing interface.

Glide Write

Glide Write (www.glidedigital.com) is part of the Glide Business suite of web-based applications. Glide Write itself is an elegant word processor that just happens to integrate seamlessly with other Glide applications, including email and chat. In addition, Glide documents can be viewed on a number of smartphones, including the iPhone, T-Mobile SideKick, and a handful of Treo and BlackBerry models.

As you can see in Figure 11.7, a Glide Write document opens in its new window. You have the normal toolbar of editing and formatting functions on top, with the document displayed below. Along the side are three tabs: Email, Share, and Chat. Click the Share tab and Glide displays a window that lets you designate which contacts you want to share with. These contacts then receive an email that includes a link to the web-based document's URL, where they can view or edit the document as desired.

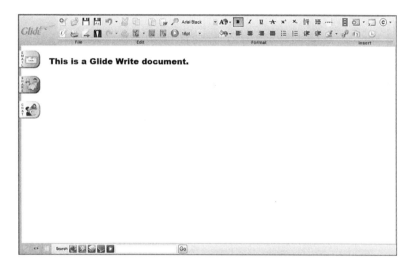

FIGURE 11.7

Editing a sharable document with Glide Write.

iNetWord

The iNetWord (www.inetword.com) web-based word processor is a full-featured application. As you can see in Figure 11.8, iNetWord features a tabbed interface, with each open document appearing on its own tab. You get support for page backgrounds, borders, page numbering, tables, images, and the like. It even comes with a number of predesigned templates for common types of documents.

For group collaboration, iNetWord lets you share individual documents or entire folders. Changes made by other users are highlighted onscreen, and it's easy to revert back to a previous version.

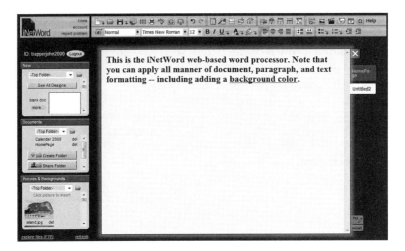

FIGURE 11.8
The tabbed interface of iNetWord.

KBdocs

As evident in Figure 11.9, KBdocs (www.kbdocs.com) is a no-frills online word processor. There are only limited formatting options, and it doesn't have any sharing or collaboration features. That said, it's probably the easiest-to-use web-based word processor, especially for newbies; just pick a username and password, click Enter, and you're ready to go.

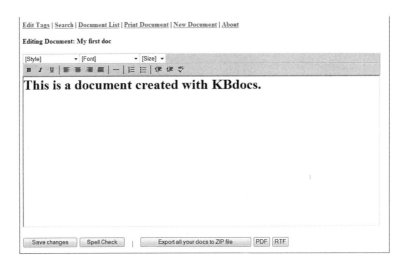

FIGURE 11.9
The minimalist interface of KBDocs.

Peepel WebWriter

Peepel WebWriter (www.peepel.com) is part of a multi-application web-based office suite. As you can see in Figure 11.10, the Peepel interface is a trifle unusual: The document you're editing appears in its own window, on top of the larger home window that holds the toolbar and tabs that you use to edit and format the document. If you can get past this little quirk, Peepel offers some interesting features, including the ability to edit your documents offline if you don't have an Internet connection.

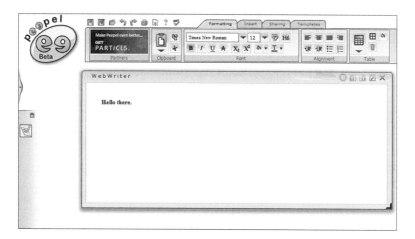

FIGURE 11.10

Peepel WebWriter's unusual interface.

Group collaboration is a snap. After you've saved a document, click the Sharing tab to see all of Peepel's sharing options. You can assign Read and Write access to different users; all you need to supply is each collaborator's email address.

ThinkFree Write

ThinkFree Write (www.thinkfree.com) is a Java-based online word processor. That lets ThinkFree mimic the Word 2003 interface, as you can see for yourself in Figure 11.11. Each new document opens in its own window, each of which has a Word-like pull-down menu and toolbar. The editing and formatting functions are also quite Word-like, complete with styles, editing marks, fields, an autocorrect function, and the like.

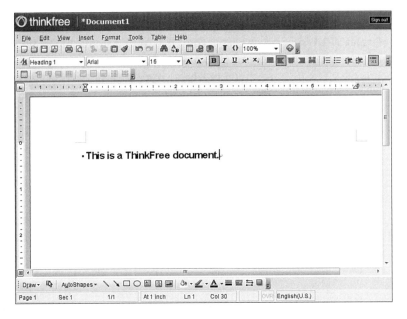

FIGURE 11.11
ThinkFree Write—a very Word-like word processor.

WriteBoard

If collaboration is your game, consider WriteBoard (www.writeboard.com), a web-based word processor designed with group collaboration in mind. WriteBoard isn't the most full-featured word processor on the web, but it does make collaboration between multiple users remarkably easy.

As you can see in Figure 11.12, WriteBoard's interface defines the term *bare bones*. It's so bare boned, in fact, that you have to enter formatting codes into the text, kind of like the way WordStar worked 25 years ago. (And who wants to do that?)

But creating pretty documents is not what WriteBoard's about. What it really is, is a wiki-style group text editor. After you create a document and share it with others, it's easy to compare different versions of the document; every time you or someone else saves an edit, a new version of the document is created and linked to in the sidebar. You can even subscribe to RSS feeds for your documents, so you'll be automatically notified of changes.

FIGURE 11.12

WriteBoard's incredibly bare-bones interface.

Zoho Writer

Zoho's web-based applications always end up being the last discussed in this book, thanks to the company's last-of-the-alphabet name. That said, Zoho is seldom the last company I think of when I'm evaluating cloud services. In most instances, Zoho is right up with Google in terms of functionality and features.

Case in point: Zoho Writer (writer.zoho.com), which easily holds its own, if not surpasses, Google Docs in the web-based word processor race. As you can see in Figure 11.13, multiple documents display in a single window, thanks to Zoho Writer's tabbed interface. You get all the standard editing and formatting features, as well as page numbering, headers and footers, footnotes and endnotes, tables of contents, and other advanced features not found in all other web-based word processors.

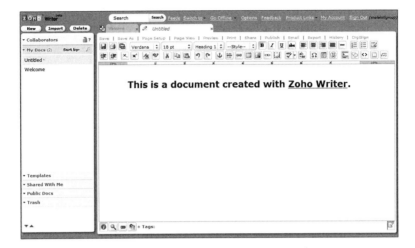

FIGURE 11.13

Zoho Writer—a full-featured web-based word processor.

Naturally, Zoho Writer offers robust sharing and collaboration features. You can share a document with individuals or with groups on either a read-only or read/write basis. Sharing is as easy as clicking the Share tab; this displays the window shown in Figure 11.14. Enter the email addresses of individuals (or the names of predefined groups), select the permission level, and then click the Share button. The chosen collaborators will receive an email inviting them to the shared document on the web.

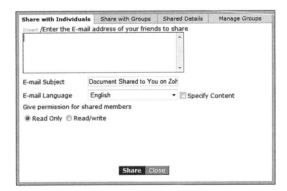

FIGURE 11.14

Sharing a document with Zoho Writer.

OFFICE SUITES IN THE CLOUD

Many of the web-based word processors featured in this chapter are parts of larger web-based office suites. These suites of applications are designed to compete with Microsoft Office and its included apps— Word, Excel, and PowerPoint—but with all the benefits of web-hosted apps and docs.

Many experts believe that web-based office suites will eventually replace traditional desktop software suites, because fewer and fewer users are working at a fixed desktop. As users become more mobile, the advantages of cloud-based applications become more notable. As long as an Internet connection is handy, web-based docs can be accessed from almost anywhere.

In addition, companies and organizations (and individuals) are starting to balk at the never-ending cost of Microsoft desktop applications. Companies pay $200 to $500 for the Office suite and are forced to upgrade every few years. Most web-based suites are free or very low cost, and are upgraded (also for free) on a continuing basis. A web-based application costs less to obtain and to maintain than Microsoft Office—and when you have hundreds or thousands of users in an organization, this kind of cost savings can't be ignored.

That said, it will take a long time for organizations to completely switch from Office to web-based alternatives. It's a matter of inertia, which rules larger organizations; it's simply a lot of trouble to switch plat-forms, even when considerable cost savings can be applied. (It also introduces challenges in sharing documents with those still using Word outside the organization.) But change does happen, albeit slowly, and the writing is on the wall. It's unlikely that the office appli-cation environment will look the same 10 years from now as it does today.

And which web-based applications will companies be switching to? You've explored some of them already in this chapter, or at least parts of the suites. Today, the most popular web-based office suites include the following:

- Glide Business (www.glidedigital.com)
- Google Docs (docs.google.com)
- Peepel Online Office (www.peepel.com)
- ThinkFree My Office (www.thinkfree.com)
- WebEx Web Office (www.weboffice.com)
- Zoho Office (office.zoho.com)

Of these suites, Google Docs has the largest installed base today; many companies, organizations, and educational institutions have already switched from Microsoft Office to Google's free web-based applications. But don't rule out any of the competing suites, nor should you expect Microsoft to sit out the cloud services revolution forever.

It might take some time to shake out, but shake out it will. Eventually, nearly all office computing will be done in the cloud.

Collaborating on Spreadsheets

In the preceding chapter, we discussed web-based word processing applications, many of which are one component of larger web-based office suites. If the word processor is the most-used office application, the spreadsheet is the second most-important app. Office users and home users alike use spreadsheets to prepare budgets, create expense reports, perform "what if" analyses, and otherwise crunch their numbers.

And thus we come to those spreadsheets in the cloud, the web-based spreadsheets that let you share your numbers with other users via the Internet. All the advantages of web-based word processors apply to web-based spreadsheets—group collaboration, anywhere/anytime access, portability, and so on. There are some neat apps here, so read on to learn more.

How Web-Based Spreadsheets Work

If you work with numbers at all, you're familiar with Microsoft Excel (or, if you're showing your age, Lotus 1-2-3 or Borland's Quattro Pro). Excel is a software program that you use to work with numbers; you enter numbers into individual cells arranged in rows and columns, and then use formulas and functions to perform calculations on those numbers.

Whereas Excel is a traditional desktop software program stored on your computer's hard disk, a web-based spreadsheet application is hosted in the cloud—as are the individual spreadsheets you create with the application. Web-based spreadsheet applications do their best to emulate the most-used features of Microsoft Excel, down to the assortment of functions, charts, and the like. So if you know how to use Excel, you'll be quite comfortable with most of the web-based spreadsheet applications discussed here.

Benefits of Web-Based Spreadsheets

A web-based spreadsheet application carries with it all the same benefits as you get with other web-based applications:

- Your spreadsheets can be accessed from any Internet-connected computer, not just the computer you originally created the spreadsheet with.

- Your spreadsheets are still accessible if you have a computer problem or hard disk crash.

- You an easily share your spreadsheets with others—enabling workgroup collaboration with users in other locations.

In addition, most web-based spreadsheets today are free—which is not the case with Microsoft Excel and the Office suite. This is especially appealing to cash-starved organizations and even large corporations looking to improve the bottom line. Free is a lot better than the hundreds of dollars per user that you'll pay for Microsoft Office.

Should You Use a Web-Based Spreadsheet?

Let's be upfront about this: A web-based spreadsheet application is not ideal for all users, especially those with sophisticated needs. That said, when does a web-based spreadsheet make sense?

Here's who I recommend take a look at these web-based applications:

- **Beginning users.** If you're just learning how to use a spreadsheet program, there's no better place to start than with a web-based application. Most of these cloud apps have slightly less functionality than the more established Microsoft Excel, which actually works to your benefit; you won't be overwhelmed by all the advanced options that clutter the Excel workspace. In addition, most of these web-based spreadsheets are extremely easy to use. Everything you need is right out in the open, not hidden beneath layers of menus and dialog boxes.

- **Casual users.** A web-based spreadsheet application is also a good choice if your number-crunching needs are somewhat modest. If all you're doing is totaling a few numbers or creating a simple budget or two, a web-based application gets the job done with ease.

- **Anyone who wants access to spreadsheets from multiple locations.** If you work on the same numbers when you travel—even between work and home—a web-based spreadsheet application is a virtual necessity. You don't have to worry about copying files from one computer to another or keeping those files synchronized; you're always accessing the same versions of your spreadsheets, stored in the cloud.

- **Anyone who needs to share spreadsheets with others.** When you want others to view the numbers you're working on, hosting your spreadsheet on the web makes it easy. You can share your spreadsheet with other team members or interested parties over the web; just authorize them to access your spreadsheet in read-only mode.

- **Anyone who needs to edit spreadsheets in a collaborative environment.** When you're working on a group project (such as a budget for a large organization), you often need multiple users to both access and edit data in a spreadsheet. This is quickly and easily accomplished via the sharing and collaboration features present in most web-based spreadsheet applications.

All that said, a web-based word spreadsheet isn't for everyone. So who *shouldn't* use one of these applications?

- **Power users.** If you've created your own custom spreadsheets in Microsoft Excel, especially those with fancy macros and pivot tables and the like, a web-based spreadsheet application is not for you. Most of these cloud applications lack Excel's most advanced features and simply won't get the job done.

- **Anyone who wants to create sophisticated printouts**. Most of today's web-based spreadsheet applications lack some of the more sophisticated formatting options that Excel users take for granted (no cell borders in spreadsheets, for example). With these web-based apps, what you see onscreen is typically what prints out—for better or for worse.

- **Anyone working on sensitive documents**. Web-based applications spreadsheets are not good tools if your company has a lot of trade secrets it wants to protect. In fact, some organizations may bar their employees from working on documents that don't reside on their own secured servers, which rules out web-based applications entirely.

- **Anyone who needs to work when not connected to the Internet**. This is the blatantly obvious one, but if you're not connected to the Internet, you can't connect to and work with a web-based application. To work offline, you need Microsoft Excel.

So, if you're a beginning or casual user who doesn't need fancy charts or printouts, or if you need to share your spreadsheets or collaborate online with other users, a web-based spreadsheet application is worth checking out.

Exploring Web-Based Spreadsheets

Several web-based spreadsheet applications are worthy competitors to Microsoft Excel. Chief among these is Google Spreadsheets, which we'll discuss first, but there are many other apps that also warrant your attention. If you're at all interested in moving your number crunching and financial analysis into the cloud, these web-based applications are worth checking out.

Google Spreadsheets

Google Spreadsheets was Google's first application in the cloud office suite first known as Google Docs & Spreadsheets and now just known as Google Docs. (It's also the only app in the suite that Google developed in-house.) As befits its longevity, Google Spreadsheets is Google's most sophisticated web-based application.

You access your existing and create new spreadsheets from the main Google Docs page (docs.google.com). To create a new spreadsheet, click the New button and select Spreadsheet; the new spreadsheet opens in a new window.

As you can see in Figure 12.1, the Google Spreadsheets workspace looks a lot like every other PC-based spreadsheet application you've ever used, whether you started with VisiCalc, 1-2-3, Quattro Pro, or Excel. You'll quickly recognize the familiar rows-and-columns grid. Sure, the buttons or links for some specific operations might be in slightly different locations, but pretty much everything you expect to find is somewhere on the page.

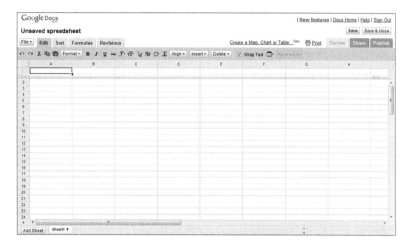

FIGURE 12.1

The tabbed interface of Google Spreadsheets.

The first thing to note is that Google Spreadsheets uses a tabbed interface and that the workspace changes slightly depending on which tab (Edit, Sort, Formulas, or Revisions) you select. Each tab in a Google spreadsheet has its own toolbar of options, specific to that toolbar's function:

- **Edit**. This tab displays a toolbar full of editing and formatting options, such as cut/copy/paste, number and text formatting, cell alignment, and the like. There's also a button on the toolbar to add a chart to your spreadsheet, based on selected data.

- **Sort**. This tab displays an abbreviated toolbar of sort-related options. You can sort the selected cells in normal or inverse order or opt to freeze the header rows for easier sorting.

- **Formulas**. This tab displays a Range Names button, which you can use to name a range of cells. There are also links to insert some of the most common functions (Sum, Count, Average, Min, Max, and Product), as well as a More link that displays all available functions.

■ **Revisions**. This final tab displays a pull-down list of the various versions of the current file. You can also use the Older and Newer buttons to switch to a different version.

The latest version of Google Spreadsheets contains much functionality lacking in the original release. For example, Google Spreadsheets now contains a raft of formulas and functions, almost as many as available with Excel; it also lets you create multiple pages within a single spreadsheet file.

You also can create charts from your spreadsheet data. To create a chart, go to the Edit tab, select the data you want to graph, and then click the Add Chart button. You now see the Create Chart window shown in Figure 12.2; select the type of chart you want to create, enter a title, make any other necessary selections, and then click the Save Chart button. The resulting chart, like the one shown in Figure 12.3, appears as a movable and sizeable object within the current spreadsheet.

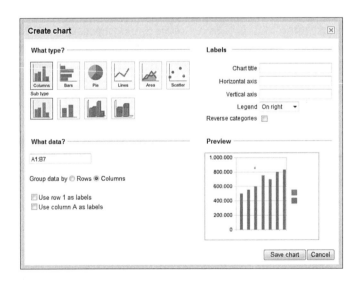

FIGURE 12.2

Creating a chart with Google Spreadsheets.

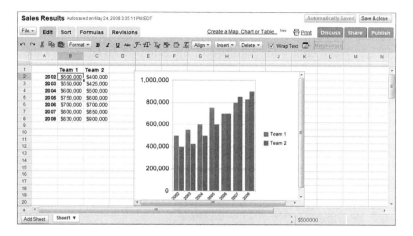

FIGURE 12.3

A chart added to a Google spreadsheet.

Of course, one of the reasons you use a web-based spreadsheet application is to share spreadsheets with other users—either for viewing or for collaborative editing. This is easy to do with Google Spreadsheets, providing that the person you want to share with has his own Google account. All you have to do is click the Share tab (at the upper-right side of the window) for that spreadsheet, and then fill in the appropriate information on the following Share This Document page. You can choose to share your spreadsheet as a read-only document (As Viewers), an editable document (As Collaborators), or as a form for other users to fill in (To Fill Out a Form).

Finally, let's take a quick look at one of the coolest and most unique features of Google Spreadsheets. Thanks to Google's willingness to let outside programmers add on to its software, many developers have created specialized gadgets that can be inserted into any spreadsheet. For example, the Gantt Chart gadget lets you graph your numbers as a basic Gantt chart. Other gadgets let you create pivot tables, generate maps from your data, and create various types of charts. To view available gadgets, click the Insert button and select Gadget.

note A gadget is a simple single-task application that can be inserted onto any web page—including the web pages that hold your Google spreadsheets.

note Learn more about Google Spreadsheets in my Digital Short Cut electronic book, *Using Google Spreadsheets*, downloadable from InformIT (www.informit.com).

In all, Google Spreadsheets is one of the most full-featured web-based spreadsheet applications available today, matching Excel almost feature to feature. It's an ideal choice for both beginning and advanced spreadsheet users.

EditGrid

If you're familiar with older versions of Microsoft Excel, EditGrid (www.editgrid.com) you'll feel quite at home with EditGrid. As you can see in Figure 12.4, the EditGrid interface is a near-replica of pre-2007 Excel, down to the tabbed sheets, pull-down menus, and toolbars. You even get 50+ keyboard shortcuts, identical to those in Excel.

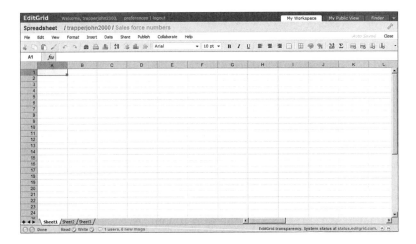

FIGURE 12.4

EditGrid—as close to Excel as you can get in a web-based app.

Its web-based nature lets EditGrid add some unique features not found in Microsoft's desktop-bound program. In addition to the expected sharing and collaboration features, EditGrid adds live chat, the ability to organize different spreadsheets and users into workspaces, and a remote data feature that lets you update your spreadsheets with real-time web data, such as stock quotes, exchange rates, and the like. The result is a powerful spreadsheet with a familiar interface—and like Google Spreadsheets, it's completely free for individual users.

eXpresso

The eXpresso online spreadsheet (www.expressocorp.com), shown in Figure
12.5, offers basic spreadsheet features paired with advanced collaboration
tools. The spreadsheet itself isn't much to write home about; there are no
functions, charts, or advanced formatting options. The collaboration features,
however, include notes, email communication, online chat, and sophisticated
sharing capabilities. This application is perhaps best used to first import existing Excel spreadsheets and then share them using eXpresso's collaboration
tools.

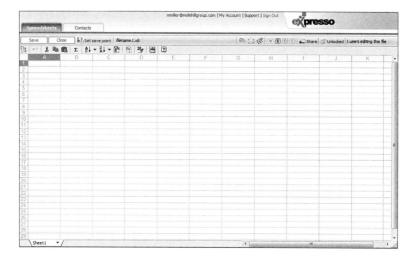

FIGURE 12.5

The basic spreadsheet interface for eXpresso.

Glide Crunch

Glide Crunch (www.glidedigital.com) is, like the Glide Write word processor,
part of the Glide Business suite of web-based applications. Glide Crunch itself
isn't web based; it's a desktop app that installs on your PC's hard drive. As
soon as you're connected to the Internet, however, Crunch gains web-based
features and automatically syncs to the Glide Webtop. It also works on the
iPhone and other mobile devices.

The Glide Crunch interface, shown in Figure 12.6, looks a little like the new
Microsoft Excel 2007 interface, using ribbon-like groups of option buttons at

the top of the screen. Crunch offers a bevy of Excel-like functions and a pivot table feature, but it doesn't (as of May 2008) let you create graphs and charts—although this feature is sure to be implemented in later versions.

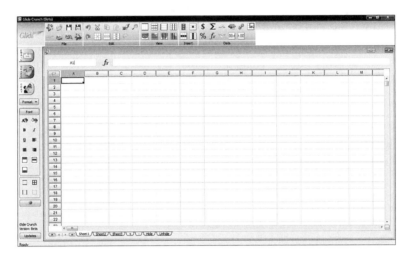

FIGURE 12.6

Glide Crunch—a combination online/offline spreadsheet.

The ability to create spreadsheets offline is a boon to users who don't always have a stable Internet connection. When you do log on to the web, you get all the benefits of a web-based app—including sharing, collaboration, and file syncing. It's certainly an approach worth considering.

Num Sum

Num Sum (www.numsum.com) is a basic web-based spreadsheet application. As you can see in Figure 12.7, there's nothing fancy here, just a typical spreadsheet workspace with editing and formatting buttons in toolbars above. Even though Num Sum does let you share and collaborate on your spreadsheets, the program includes no built-in functions and only three rudimentary chart types (line, bar, area), which makes it less than ideal for advanced spreadsheet users.

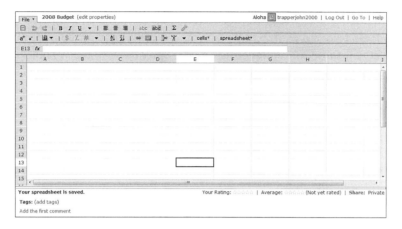

FIGURE 12.7
Num Sum's rudimentary spreadsheet interface.

Peepel WebSheet

In Chapter 11, "Collaborating on Word Processing," we discussed Peepel
WebWriter, the word processing component of the Peepel Online Office suite
(www.peepel.com). The spreadsheet component of the suite is called Peepel
WebSheet, and it works a lot like its word processing sibling.

As you can see in Figure 12.8, the spreadsheet you're editing appears in its own
window, on top of the larger home window that holds the toolbar and tabs
that you use to edit and format the spreadsheet. Yep, it's the same quirky interface found in Peepel WebWriter; it's just the way Peepel chooses to do things.

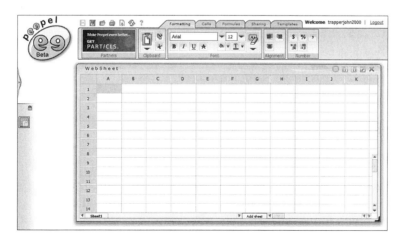

FIGURE 12.8
The quirky interface of Peepel WebSheet.

While WebSheet offers a nice selection of functions and formatting options, it doesn't have a chart feature, so you can't display your data visually. It does let you share and collaborate on your spreadsheets, but it's not the most full-featured spreadsheet application available.

Sheetster

Sheetster (www.sheetster.com) is a web-based spreadsheet written in JavaScript. Not that that matters, but it's tough to find much else to say about this app, shown in Figure 12.9. Although Sheetster does offer sharing and collaboration features, it's about as bare boned a spreadsheet as you can get. And whereas the ability to syndicate a spreadsheet via RSS is neat, it's so lacking in basic features (no charts and only rudimental formatting) that even casual users will find it frustrating.

FIGURE 12.9
Sheetster—another basic web-based spreadsheet.

ThinkFree Calc

ThinkFree Calc (www.thinkfree.com), like its ThinkFree Write sibling, is a Java-based online application. That lets ThinkFree offer a near-replica of the pre-2007 Excel interface, as you can see in Figure 12.10. Each new spreadsheet opens in its own window. Use the toolbar buttons and pull-down menus to edit and format your spreadsheets.

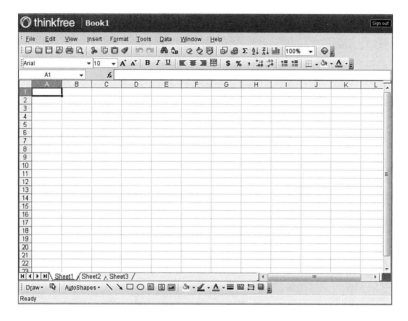

FIGURE 12.10

The Excel-like interface of ThinkFree Calc, a full-featured web-based spreadsheet.

Unlike some of the previous applications, ThinkFree Calc is a full-featured spreadsheet program. You get lots of functions (300+), full formatting features, and a wide array of charts and graphs. It's just like using Excel, except on the web.

Sharing is accomplished via ThinkFree's My Office Webtop, shown in Figure 12.11. Just pull down the menu next to the filename and select Share; you're then prompted for the names of your desired viewers or collaborators (all of whom must be fellow ThinkFree users, of course). Those users can then access the spreadsheet via their own Webtop pages.

FIGURE 12.11
Sharing files via ThinkFree's My Office Webtop.

Zoho Sheet

Zoho Sheet (sheet.zoho.com) is Zoho's web-based spreadsheet application. Like all Zoho apps, this one is full featured with great sharing and collaboration features.

As you can see in Figure 12.12, it is a lot like Google Spreadsheets. You get an Excel-like toolbar-based interface, multiple sheets in each file, a full load of functions, lots of different types of graphs, and all the formatting options you need to create great-looking printouts. The leftmost pane displays all your spreadsheet files, including those you've chosen to share with others. You can share your spreadsheets on either a read-only or read/write basis. You can also easily share files direct with designated groups of users.

Just as useful, Zoho Sheet enables you to export your web spreadsheets as Excel XLS format files, as well as files in a variety of other formats. You can also easily publish your web spreadsheets to your own website or blog; it's a simple one-button operation.

In short, even though Zoho Sheets comes last in the order of all these cloud spreadsheets, it's among the first in terms of features and functionality. It's definitely worth considering—especially if you have use for the other applications in the Zoho Office suite.

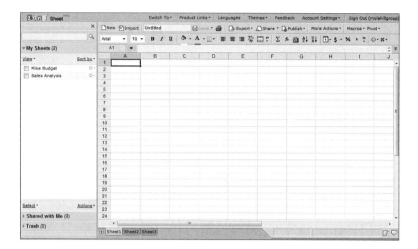

FIGURE 12.12

Last but not least, Zoho Sheet—a full-featured online spreadsheet application.

SHARING OFFICE DOCUMENTS ONLINE

You don't have to use a web-based application to share your documents online. If you're a die-hard Microsoft Office user, it's good to know that Microsoft now lets you share any Office document via its Office Live Workspace tool.

Office Live Workspace (workspace.office.live.com) enables any user to store a thousand or so Office documents online, for free. When the software extension is installed on your PC, you can easily upload and share your documents from within Microsoft Word, Excel, and Power-Point. You can even use Office Live Workspace to synchronize your Outlook contacts, tasks, and events between different computers.

Your uploaded documents are accessed from your main workspace, shown in Figure 12.13. From here, you can download documents to another computer or click the Share button to share selected documents (or your complete workspace) with other Office Live Workspace users.

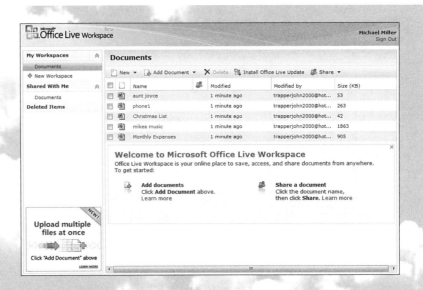

FIGURE 12.13
Microsoft Office Live Workspace—a way to share Office documents online without switching to a different web-based application.

Office Live Workspace offers web-based document storage and sharing without the need for web-based apps. It's a great way for Office users to share critical documents and group projects between multiple users. (Learn more about Office Live Workspace and other web-based file-sharing services in Chapter 15, "Storing and Sharing Files and Other Online Content.")

Collaborating on Databases

I t used to be that the big three office applications were word processing, spreadsheets, and databases. It's possible that databases have fallen from the top three (replaced either by email or presentation applications, depending on how you look at things), but large businesses especially still have plenty of need for database management applications.

In the past, a large database had to be housed onsite, typically on a large server. That limited database access to users either located in the same physical location or connected to the company's internal database—and excluded, in most instances, traveling workers and users in remote offices. This, in turn, limited the usefulness of the data contained in the database.

Today, thanks to cloud computing technology, the underlying data of a database can be stored in the cloud—on collections of web servers—instead of housed in a single physical location. This enables users both inside and outside the company to access the same data, day or night, which increases the usefulness of that data. It's a way to make data universal.

Understanding Database Management

Before we start looking at web-based database management applications, it helps to know a little about how databases themselves work. Although it's convenient to think of a database as simply a collection of data, there's more to it than just that.

How Databases Work

A database does many of the same things that a spreadsheet does, but in a different and often more efficient manner. In fact, many small businesses use spreadsheets for database-like functions.

Think of it this way. If a spreadsheet is a giant list, a database is a giant filing cabinet. Each "filing cabinet" is actually a separate database file, and contains individual index cards (called *records*) filled with specific information (arranged in *fields*).

You can use a database application to create and store anything that includes a large amount of data. For example, you can create a database that contains all your favorite recipes or the contents of your CD or video collection.

For businesses, databases tend to house large amounts of granular data— information about customers, employees, and sales. A database management program not only stores this data but also automates data entry, retrieval, and analysis. Many businesses build custom applications around their databases, so that the database itself becomes somewhat transparent. Users see only the front end that pulls information from the database.

How Online Databases Work

A local database is one in which all the data is stored on an individual computer. A networked database is one in which the data is stored on a computer or server connected to a network, and accessible by all computers connected to that network. Finally, an online or web-based database stores data on a cloud of servers somewhere on the Internet, which is accessible by any authorized user with an Internet connection.

The primary advantage of a web-based database is that data can easily be shared with a large number of other users, no matter where they may be located. When your employee database is in the cloud, for example, the human resources department in your Alaska branch can access employee information as easily as can the HR staff in Chicago—as can HR managers traveling across the country to various college job fairs.

And, because the data itself is stored in the cloud, when someone at one location updates a record, everyone accessing the database sees the new data. Synchronization is not an issue.

With these advantages in mind, most online databases are oriented toward quick information sharing among members of workgroups who've assembled to attack a project for a month or two. When accessing data in this manner, ease of use is paramount, which most of these cloud applications address with simple and intuitive interfaces.

Exploring Web-Based Databases

In the desktop computing world, the leading database program today is Microsoft Access. (This wasn't always the case; dBase used to rule the database roost, but things change over time.) In larger enterprises, you're likely to encounter more sophisticated software from Microsoft, Oracle, and other companies.

Interestingly, none of the major database software developers currently provide web-based database applications. Instead, you have to turn to a handful of start-up companies (and one big established name) for your online database needs.

Blist

One of the newest entrants in the web-based database market is Blist (www.blist.com). Blist is a relatively easy-to-use database designed for nontechnical businesspeople; in fact, the company bills it as something of a cross between a spreadsheet and database program.

Not surprisingly, the default Blist interface uses a spreadsheet metaphor, as you can see in Figure 13.1, complete with rows and columns. That said, you can switch to a forms-based interface, shown in Figure 13.2, which is perhaps better for entering raw data one record at a time.

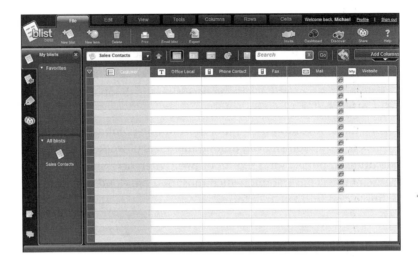

FIGURE 13.1

Blist's default spreadsheet-like interface.

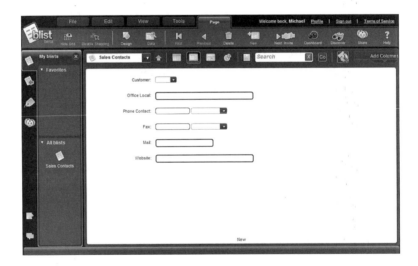

FIGURE 13.2

Another way to enter data, with Blist's form view.

Despite its ease of use, Blist provides some robust database management and reporting capabilities. You can make your data completely public or share it with designated users. Databases can be read-only, or users can have the option of adding new records or deleting old ones.

Cebase

Cebase (www.cebase.com) lets you create new database applications with a few clicks of your mouse; all you have to do is fill in a few forms and make a few choices from some pull-down lists. Data entry is via web forms, and then your data is displayed in a spreadsheet-like layout, as shown in Figure 13.3. You can then sort, filter, and group your data as you like.

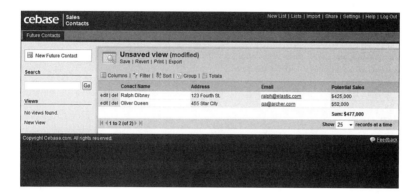

FIGURE 13.3

Viewing data in a Cebase database.

Sharing is accomplished by clicking the Share link at the top of any data page. You invite users to share your database via email, and then adjust their permissions after they've accepted your invitation.

Dabble DB

Similar to Cebase is Dabble DB (www.dabbledb.com). Like Cebase, Dabble DB makes it easy to create new databases and add new records. Your data can be displayed in a number of different views, including the spreadsheet-like table view shown in Figure 13.4. You can then sort, group, and filter your data; create various types of reports; and use your data to generate graphs, calendars, and maps.

Dabble DB offers three ways to share your data. The Pages option enables you to collect data from other users without granting access to the underlying database. The Users option lets other users access the raw data in the database. And the Schema option uses the Dabble DB JavaScript API to let others interact with your data on other websites.

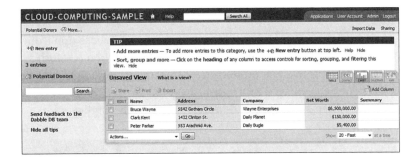

FIGURE 13.4
Viewing data in a Dabble DB database.

Lazybase

Lazybase (www.lazybase.com) is a simple online database, better suited for individuals than for large businesses. Creating a new database is as easy as filling in a few forms, as shown in Figure 13.5. Adding new records is just as easy. Your data is then presented on a clean, easy-to-grasp web page. Although there aren't a lot of fancy reports and such, Lazybase does offer simple data entry and display—easy enough for most home users to grasp.

FIGURE 13.5
Creating a new Lazybase database.

One of the nice features about Lazybase is that the simple databases you create can be shared with anyone you like. You can also import them into any website. In addition, Lazybase offers RSS feed subscription, and the ability to create custom bookmarklets so that you can instantly save data from any web page to your database.

MyWebDB

The application called myWebDB (hu.oneteamtech.com/mywebdb.html) is billed as a do-it-yourself Web 2.0 database application. Like the other web-based databases discussed in this chapter, myWebDB lets you create powerful applications by using its Builder Wizard to fill in a few forms, no coding necessary.

The myWebDB application then designs an application to match your data needs. The applications generated by myWebDB feature good-looking interfaces, complete with navigation menus, editable data grids, and intuitive data entry screens, like the one shown in Figure 13.6.

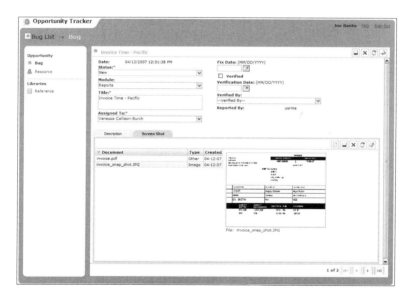

FIGURE 13.6

Entering data into a myWebDB web form.

QuickBase

QuickBase (quickbase.intuit.com) is one of the oldest and most feature-rich online databases available today. Because it comes from Intuit, the company behind Quicken and Quickbooks, it's also one of the most stable and reliable web-based applications you can find.

It's so sophisticated, in fact, that Intuit doesn't even bill it as a database management program. Instead, Intuit says that QuickBase is a "website that lets you quickly and easily select, customize and share online workgroup applications that actually work the way your teams do." And just what is a "workgroup application?" Again, from Intuit: "An online workgroup application is a web-based solution that helps a team organize, track and share information—which in turn improves team productivity." Kind of a fancy way of saying that QuickBase lets you design your own web-based database applications.

You can get started with QuickBase by using one of the application's ready-made applications, and then customize that application to suit your own specific needs. If there's no appropriate existing application, you can create a new one from scratch.

Each application has its own form-based entry and table-based views. You can then generate the necessary reports or share your data with other users. You even get customizable dashboards for each application, like the one in Figure 13.7, the better to view key data at a glance.

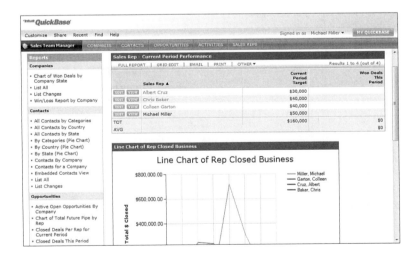

FIGURE 13.7

A QuickBase application management dashboard.

As you can probably tell, QuickBase's functionality is head and shoulders above most web-based database applications. Of course, you pay for this sophistication; unlike other cloud applications, QuickBase is not free. Pricing is on a per-user basis, starting at $249 per month for 10 users and going up from there. But if your needs are such that simple databases won't do, QuickBase is well worth the expense.

TeamDesk

TeamDesk (www.teamdesk.net) is, like QuickBase, a powerful web-based database management application that facilitates advanced application development. You can work from predefined applications for many business functions or create your own custom apps.

The TeamDesk Application Library includes applications for project management, marketing, sales, customer support, human resources, billing, and other business functions. For example, Figure 13.8 shows a sales contracts tracking application, with data displayed in tabular format.

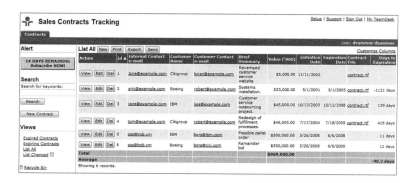

FIGURE 13.8

One of the predefined business applications available in the TeamDesk Application Library.

Trackvia

Trackvia (www.trackvia.com) is similar to TeamDesk, in that it lets you create your databases from dozens of sample applications or completely from scratch. You can choose to view several predefined reports for each database application or generate a custom report. To create a custom report, you use the web page shown in Figure 13.9. Just select the columns you want to include and how you want your results sorted.

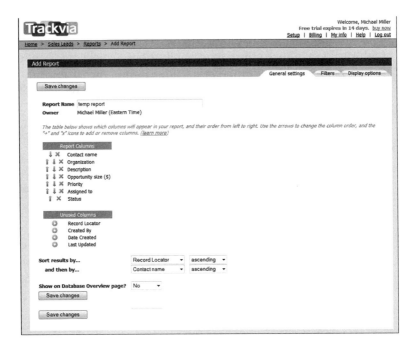

FIGURE 13.9
Generating a custom report with Trackvia.

Trackvia enables you to generate forms you can display on your own website and thus let your site's users enter data on their own. You can also share your databases with designated users; you assign different levels of permission, from Add (enter new records only) to View to Edit (change existing data) to Delete.

Zoho Creator

Zoho offers two different database products: Zoho Creator and Zoho DB & Reports. Of the two, Zoho Creator is the easiest to use and best suited for casual users.

Zoho Creator (creator.zoho.com) is a versatile data repository, complete with data-entry forms and spreadsheet-like list views. While easy to use, Zoho Creator is robust enough to let you create your own simple database applications.

It's easy enough to create a new database; you can start from scratch or use a predesigned template. You enter new data into a web form, like the one shown in Figure 13.10. You can then display your data in a number of different views, including summary, table, and spreadsheet views. You can even create web forms for data entry and embed them in your website or blog.

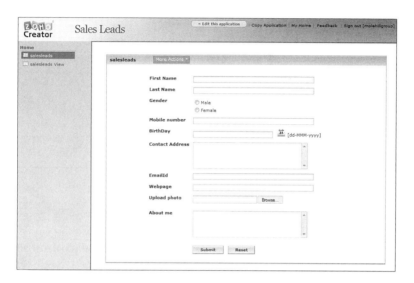

FIGURE 13.10

Entering data into a Zoho Creator form.

Zoho DB & Reports

If your database needs are more robust, turn to Zoho DB & Reports (db.zoho.com). Zoho DB offers more in-depth reporting than is available with Zoho Creator, including charts, pivot tables, and other report types. (Figure 13.11 shows a sample chart generated with Zoho DB.) In addition, Zoho DB supports web-based APIs that enable it to serve as a back end for your own hosted applications; it also supports SQL for more robust data queries.

Like Zoho Creator, Zoho DB can be accessed from any Internet-connected computer. You can also share your data and reports for collaborative development and analysis and embed your reports into your own website.

In short, if your needs are simple, use Zoho Creator. If your needs are more complex, or if you're accustomed to working with Access, SQL Server, and similar relational database management programs, go with Zoho DB & Reports.

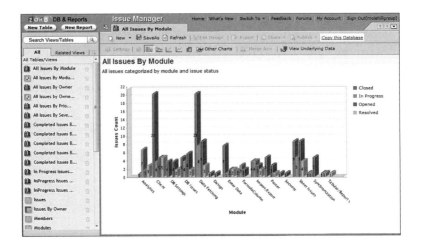

FIGURE 13.11

A sophisticated chart generated by Zoho DB & Reports.

EVALUATING ONLINE DATABASES

When you're trying to decide which online database to use, it seems as if there's QuickBase and then there's everything else. That's because QuickBase has been around longer than most of the competition, is offered by an established software company (Intuit), and is targeted at large companies. Not all of QuickBase's competitors have the same lineage, level of technical support, and goals.

I certainly recommend that you consider QuickBase, especially if you're working for a large company or organization and have correspondingly sophisticated database needs. QuickBase should also be on your short list if you want to develop specialized applications that use the data from a large database.

If your needs are more modest, however, a number of the applications discussed in this chapter are worth considering. I'm particularly partial to Zoho's two offerings, Creator (for smaller needs) and DB & Reports (for larger databases and more sophisticated applications). I also like Bliss, especially for the nontechnical users among us, although several of the other web-based applications can provide similar functionality.

Bottom line, there are a lot of differences between the web-based database applications available today. The most basic applications are easy to use but limited in functionality; the more sophisticated applications have a steeper learning curve but offer more sophisticated reporting with more advanced automation. Choose your application wisely—you don't want to end up with an underpowered app or one that's too difficult for your organization to use.

Collaborating on Presentations

O
ne of the last components of the traditional office suite to move into the cloud is the presentation application. Microsoft PowerPoint has ruled the desktop forever, and it's proven difficult to offer competitive functionality in a web-based application; if nothing else, slides with large graphics are slow to upload and download in an efficient manner.

That said, there is a new crop of web-based presentation applications that aim to give PowerPoint a run for its money. The big players, as might be expected, are Google and Zoho, but there are several other applications that are worth considering if you need to take your presentations with you on the road—or collaborate with users in other locations.

Preparing Presentations Online

Working with an online presentation application is no different from working with any other web-based application. Users from multiple locations can access the presentation directly from any Internet-connected computer, making it easy to assemble a presentation via group collaboration. This is becoming an essential feature, as more and more presentations for large organizations are created by multiple people from different departments or disciplines. For example, you may have one piece of the presentation created by the marketing department, another by the accounting or finance department, and another by the sales department. With the desktop-bound PowerPoint, this would require the passing around (via email) and synchronizing of on or more PowerPoint files. With a web-based app, each department can work on its part of the master file simultaneously—even if it's not in the same physical location or time zone.

Another benefit from using a web-based presentation program is that you don't have to worry about loading the presentation file onto your notebook, taking it with you to a remote meeting site, and connecting your equipment to the room's projector and other hardware. Instead, you can use a PC provided by the meeting site and just connect to the web to access your presentation; you don't even have to take your notebook with you.

Most web-based presentation programs even let you import your existing PowerPoint presentations. This is great if you've already created a presentation or template that you want to reuse in the future; you can then give your existing presentation from the web.

The only problem with some web-based presentation applications is that you don't always have the same range of graphics, transitions, and effects available to you as you do with PowerPoint. (PowerPoint is a very full-featured program.) So you want to be sure you're comfortable with the options available before you switch from PowerPoint to a web-based alternative.

Evaluating Web-Based Presentation Applications

Unlike some other application categories, there is no clear-cut leader in the web-based presentation market. Some users like Google Presentations, some like Zoho Show, some have other favorites. So take a careful look at the following applications and choose the one that offers the right features for your needs.

BrinkPad

BrinkPad (www.brinkpad.com) is a Java applet that works inside any web browser. It lets you create, save, and publish your presentations and slide shows on the web. It also lets others share and collaborate on your presentations.

The BrinkPad interface, shown in Figure 14.1, is fairly intuitive. But it doesn't offer much in the way of predesigned templates, offers no slide transition effects, and doesn't include charting or table tools. You do get rudimentary drawing tools, however, which enable you to mix illustrations, text, and imported digital pictures. So BrinkPad's limited functionality means that it's not yet a satisfactory replacement for PowerPoint.

FIGURE 14.1
The easy-to-use interface for BrinkPad.

Empressr

Empressr (www.empressr.com) offers more functionality than BrinkPad and similar applications, via an interface that should be somewhat familiar to PowerPoint users. You can insert text, shapes, tables, or charts onto any slide. You can even create custom slide backgrounds.

As you can see in Figure 14.2, Empressr lets you create charts, which many web-based presentation apps don't. You also get a range of slide transition effects, something else you don't find with many competing applications.

These features make Empressr the application of choice for heavy PowerPoint users wanting to make the switch to a web-based application.

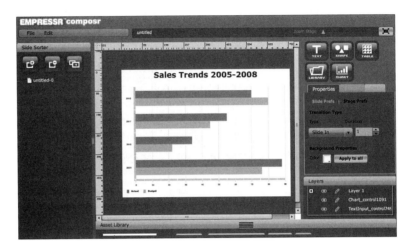

FIGURE 14.2
Creating a new slide with Empressr, complete with chart and transition effect.

Google Presentations

If there's a leader in the online presentations market, it's probably Google Presentations, simply because of Google's dominant position with other web-based office apps. Google Presentations is the latest addition to the Google Docs suite of apps, joining the Google Docs word processor and Google Spreadsheets spreadsheet application.

Users can create new presentations and open existing ones from the main Google Docs page (docs.google.com). Open a presentation by clicking its title or icon. Create a new presentation by selecting New, then Presentation. Your presentation now opens in a new window on your desktop.

As you can see in Figure 14.3, the Google Presentations interface looks a lot like older versions of PowerPoint, but with a few features missing. In particular, although you include text, images, and shapes on a slide, there's no chart-making facility. In addition, Google Presentations at present doesn't offer any slide animations.

FIGURE 14.3

Editing slides with Google Presentations.

What you do get is the ability to add title, text, and blank slides; a PowerPoint-like slide sorter pane; a selection of predesigned themes (shown in Figure 14.4); the ability to publish your file to the web or export as a PowerPoint PPT or Adobe PDF file; and quick and easy sharing and collaboration, the same as with Google's other web-based apps.

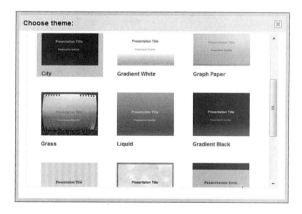

FIGURE 14.4

Some predesigned slide themes in Google Presentations.

If you use the other Google Docs apps, Google Presentations should be a natural choice. However, the lack of advanced presentation features might cause power PowerPoint users to look elsewhere for their online presentation needs.

Preezo

If you're looking to a slightly more full-featured alternative to Google Presentations, check out Preezo (www.preezo.com). Although Preezo, like Google Presentations, doesn't offer chart creation, it does add a bevy of slide transition effects.

As you can see in Figure 14.5, Preezo even looks a lot like Google Presentations. You get the obligatory slide sorter in the leftmost pane, the current slide in the main window, and all available editing and formatting options in a toolbar and series of pull-down menus. Slide transition effects include wipes, fades, splits, and pushes.

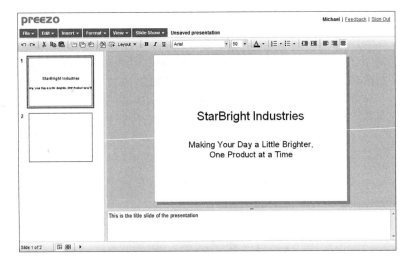

FIGURE 14.5

Editing a Preezo presentation.

Presentation Engine

Presentation Engine (www.presentationengine.com) is an advanced presentation program with an eye toward snazzy graphics and transition effects. It offers a level of graphics sophistication not found in competing online applications.

You start by selecting a design style from the list shown in Figure 14.6. You then choose background music and a color scheme for your presentation, and then start adding the text for your slides. The result is a multimedia presentation, like the one in Figure 14.7, saved as an executable file that can be run from the web or downloaded to your PC.

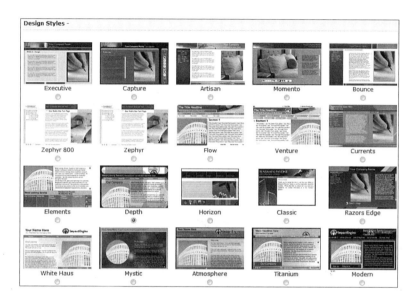

FIGURE 14.6

Choosing a Presentation Engine design style.

FIGURE 14.7

A finished Presentation Engine multimedia presentation.

What you don't get with Presentation Engine is a lot of flexibility. Want to add a chart? You can't. Want to vary from the suggestion slide transitions and animations? You can't. But if you like Presentation Engine's visual flair, you should be satisfied with the quality of the results.

PreZentit

PreZentit (www.prezentit.com) is a slick-looking application that offers features not found with competing programs. You get a library of graphics you can use for slide backgrounds, a bevy of slide transition effects (shown in Figure 14.8) and easy sharing and collaboration with authorized users. What you don't get is a chart-creation function, but then again, most competing applications don't have that either.

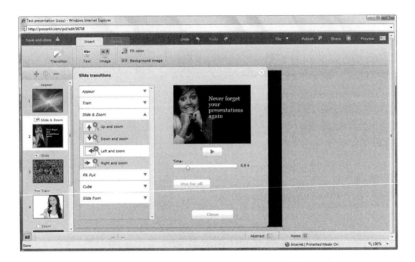

FIGURE 14.8
The slide transition effects available with PreZentit.

The presentations you create with PreZentit are saved in HTML format. You can run your presentations from the web or download to your PC for offline viewing.

SlideRocket

SlideRocket (www.sliderocket.com) is one of the newest web-based presentation applications. As you can see in Figure 14.9, SlideRocket offers an appealing interface with lots of advanced features.

FIGURE 14.9

SlideRocket—one of the most advanced web-based presentation applications.

You get a lot of features in SlideRocket that aren't available in competing applications. For example, SlideRocket offers predesigned static and motion themes; slide transitions and builds; a variety of 3D effects; the ability to import audio, video, and animations on your slides; a powerful chart creator; and group collaboration and presentation building. You can then present your work via the web in real time or download your presentations for offline use.

If you're a power PowerPoint user or just have advanced needs, SlideRocket is definitely worth checking out.

ThinkFree Show

ThinkFree Show (www.thinkfree.com) is the presentation component of ThinkFree's suite of office applications. As you can see in Figure 14.10, Show looks a lot like pre-2007 PowerPoint, minus the charting function. You do, however, get both slide transition effects and custom animations for text and objects on a slide, as well as the ability to inset tables and shapes.

Sharing is accomplished via ThinkFree's My Office Webtop, which is also where you share other types of ThinkFree documents. You can share presentations for viewing only or for group editing, and then play back your presentations from any Internet-connected computer.

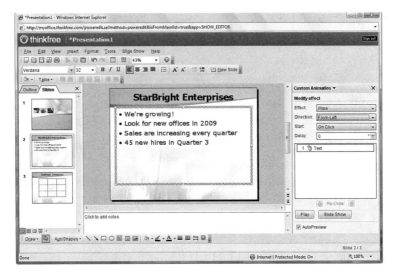

FIGURE 14.10
The PowerPoint-like interface of ThinkFree Show.

Thumbstacks

Thumbstacks (www.thumbstacks.com) is a bare-bones online presentation program. The interface is easy enough to use, as you can see in Figure 14.11, but you're pretty much limited to plain text slides; there are no tables, charts, or transition effects.

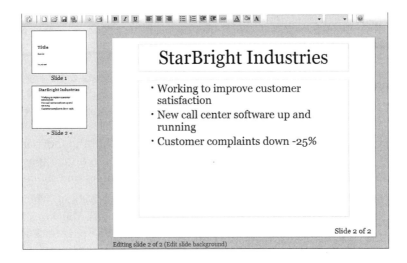

FIGURE 14.11
The bare-bones interface of Thumbstacks.

Zoho Show

Zoho Show (show.zoho.com), shown in Figure 14.12, is probably the weakest link in the Zoho Office suite. Like Google Presentations, Zoho Show lets you create good-looking text-based slides, but that's about all. There is no chart-creation function, no tables, and no slide transition effects.

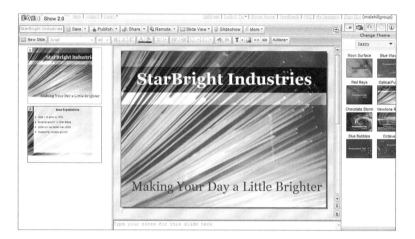

FIGURE 14.12

The Zoho Show web-based presentation program.

That said, Zoho Show integrates well with Zoho's other web-based applications and offers easy sharing and collaboration. So if you want a good basic presentation with few bells or whistles, it's worth checking out.

SHARING YOUR POWERPOINT PRESENTATIONS

There's one more class of web-based applications we need to discuss in this chapter. If you already have a PowerPoint presentation and just want to share it with others via the web, you might be interested in a presentation-sharing site. These sites, such as SlideBurner (www.slide-burner.com) and SlideShare (www.slideshare.net), work kind of like YouTube, but for presentations rather than videos.

These sites, like YouTube, are file-sharing communities that are free for anyone to use. Once you sign up, you can upload any presentation in PPT (PowerPoint), PDF, or ODP (OpenOffice) format. The presentations you upload are then made available to the site's community; you can make your presentations private (viewable by invitation only) or public (meaning anyone can see them).

Of course, you can also use these sites to host the presentations you give on the road or broadcast to remote colleagues. Just send the URL for your uploaded presentation to your colleagues or enter it into your own web browser. Your presentation can then be viewed in its default viewing window or, on most sites, full screen.

A presentation sharing site makes sense if you don't want to switch from PowerPoint to a web-based application but still need to share your final presentation with others in remote locations. It's also a good idea if you want to give a presentation on the road but don't want to haul your notebook with you, or even if you just want a backup while you're traveling. What you can't do, of course, is edit the presentations you upload; these services are for sharing, not for collaboration.

Storing and Sharing Files and Other Online Content

Cloud computing isn't just about accessing applications over the web. The cloud can also be used to store documents, either as a giant backup drive or as your primary source of file storage.

In addition, you can use the cloud to store and share your favorite websites. By putting your favorites online, you can share them with all your friends—no email or instant messaging necessary. (When stored on the cloud, you can also access your favorites when you're using another computer, which is great when you're traveling or out of the office.)

Read on, then, to learn more about these two similar but different ways to store things in the cloud.

Understanding Cloud Storage

The first form of web-based data storage we'll examine is called *cloud storage*. This is a form of networked data storage where data files are stored on multiple virtual servers.

> **note** One terabyte equals 1,000 gigabytes, and 1 petabyte equals 1,000 terabytes.

What Is Cloud Storage?

The servers used for cloud storage are typically hosted by third-party companies who operate large data centers. When you subscribe to a cloud storage service, you lease storage capacity from the cloud storage service. You then have access to the contracted amount of storage space, which you access via the Internet.

What you see looks like a single server or hard disk, but it's really just a virtual server. In reality, your data may be stored across multiple servers, sometimes spanning multiple locations (or even continents!) that then appear to be a single server in your storage dashboard.

> **note** I like the way Geoff Tudor, the co-founder of cloud storage provider Nirvanix, describes cloud storage. He compares cloud storage to electrical service: When you turn on a light switch, you don't know exactly from where each individual electron originates. The same applies to stored data in the cloud—although you might not know where that data is physically stored, all you care about is that you have access to that data.

Know that true cloud storage is massive. We're not talking mere gigabytes and terabytes, as you might find on a desktop PC or web server. Instead, a cloud storage service might offer multiple petabytes of storage.

The best-known cloud storage service today is probably Amazon.com's Simple Storage Service (S3). Cloud storage is also offers by many other companies, with services either planned or rumored from IBM, Google, and EMC.

Why Use Cloud Storage?

Why is cloud storage such a big deal—especially to large companies? There are three primary benefits to cloud storage:

- **Scalability**. When you rent cloud storage space, you can opt to use as much or as little space as you need. It's easy to "flip and switch" and increase your storage space if you suddenly have larger storage needs. You don't have to buy the additional computers required to house the extra data, but rather can use more of the space available in the cloud (and feel free to use as much space as you need).

■ **Reliability**. If you've ever had your company's server go down, you know how important it is to have access to backup data. Well, cloud storage can be used as giant online backup drive. Even if you rely on cloud services for your primary data storage, you still have the peace of mind that comes from knowing your data is duplicated on multiple servers.

■ **Lower costs**. How much do you pay per terabyte of storage? Even with hard disk prices coming down, it's still cheaper to use the virtual servers in the cloud. Cloud storage services can offer lower storage rates because they more efficiently use the server space they have; space gets reassigned to users almost instantly, on an as-needed basis.

It's a lot cheaper to use excess space in the cloud than it is to purchase a new server or hard disk drive.

Risks of Storing Data in the Clouds

Of course, some risk is associated with using cloud storage services. Let's look at the most talked-about issues:

■ **Reliability**. Remember when I said cloud storage is more reliable than traditional physical storage? That might not always be the case. What do you do when your cloud service provider has technical problems and either goes offline (which means you can't access your data) or actually loses stored data? It's happened before. Amazon had a well-publicized outage of its storage service in February 2008. If a cloud storage service doesn't have adequate infrastructure or doesn't maintain multiple backups, your data could be at risk.

■ **Security**. While all cloud storage providers tout how secure their systems are, there still exists the possibility that high-tech thieves could break into the system and view or steal your sensitive data. It's almost always less safe to store your data elsewhere than where you have physical control over it.

■ **User error**. Not all reliability security issues originate with the cloud storage provider. Given that you employ fallible human beings to manage your systems, it's not inconceivable that someone could inadvertently let a password slip, or enter an incorrect web address. All it takes is one simple mistake to expose your data to unauthorized users or permanently delete data you don't want to delete.

> ▪ **Access problems**. Because you're accessing your data over an Internet connection, you're in big trouble if that connection goes down—either on your end or with your cloud storage provider. And the connection doesn't have to go completely down to cause problems; latency in accessing data is an issue with any Internet connection, even the fastest ones. Slow connections, of course, present problems of their own, in terms of time it takes to upload and download files.

With all these caveats in place, it makes sense to back up data in at least two places, and not rely exclusively on the cloud for all your storage needs. Whatever you store in the cloud should also be stored somewhere more accessible, for safety's sake.

Evaluating Online File-Storage and -Sharing Services

Where online can you store your valuable data? Let's look at some of the more popular cloud storage services—many of which also offer file-sharing capabilities.

Amazon S3

The Amazon Simple Storage Service (S3) provides unlimited online storage. You access your stored data via a simple web interface. S3 launched in March 2006, making it one of the most established online storage services in today's market.

Amazon charges fees for the amount of data stored and for the bandwidth used in uploading and downloading that data. In the United States, you pay $0.15 per gigabyte of storage used, plus a data transfer fee that ranges between $0.10 and $0.17 per gigabyte transferred.

One of the selling points for S3 is that it uses the same scalable storage infrastructure that Amazon.com uses to run its own global e-commerce website. You access Amazon S3 by going to aws.amazon.com and clicking the Amazon Simple Storage Service link.

Egnyte

Egnyte (www.egnyte.com) provides online file storage, backup, and sharing. You can easily designate authorized users with whom to share specific files and folders, complete with automatic file versioning.

Access to the Egnyte service is via the simple web interface you see in Figure 15.1. You set up a virtual online file server that you configure according to your specific needs. You can then designate shared folders and subfolders with different permissions for power users and standard users. Uploading files is as easy as clicking a few buttons. Anything you upload to your shared folders can then be shared with other users you authorize.

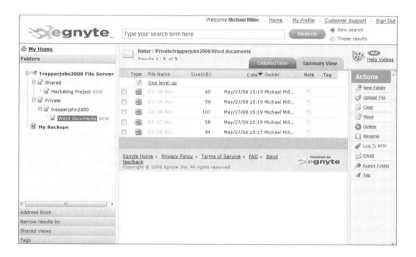

FIGURE 15.1

Managing uploaded files with Egnyte.

ElephantDrive

ElephantDrive (www.elephantdrive.com) is a user-friendly online file-storage service. They offer three different versions of different-sized users: Home Edition, Pro Edition, and Pro Plus Edition. Each edition has different storage and transfer limits. The Home Edition is priced at an affordable $9.95/month.

Microsoft Office Live Workspace

We first discussed Microsoft Office Live Workspace (workspace.office.live.com) back in Chapter 12, "Collaborating on Spreadsheets." Think of Live Workspace as a specialized cloud storage service; you can use it to store Microsoft Office documents and Office documents only. In addition, you're limited to the number of documents you can store, typically around 1,000 per user.

The nice thing about Office Live Workspace is that it's free—although you do need to own the Microsoft Office suite to create your Office documents, of course.

This makes it a great way to store your main or backup copies of your Word, Excel, and PowerPoint documents. You can also access your documents from any location, whether you're in the office, at home, or on the road. What you can't do, however, is store non-Office documents, which makes it a rather limited data-storage service.

Mosso

Mosso (www.mosso.com) is a business-ready cloud hosting platform. Both storage and bandwidth scale automatically as needed; you pay on a per-gigabyte basis for what you actually use.

You can use Mosso to host anything from individual files to complete websites. In fact, Mosso let you serve as your own website hosting service, complete with domain registration and client billing services.

note If you want to share live documents and the contents of your computer desktop with a small group of coworkers or friends, check out Microsoft SharedView (connect.microsoft.com/site/sitehome.aspx?SiteID=94). Not a cloud application per se, SharedView is a remote desktop and conferencing system that lets you show and share documents (and chat) with up to 15 people at once. Each participant installs the SharedView software on his or her PC; when you start a session, each client communicates with the others using IM-like technology. (In fact, SharedView works with Windows Live Messenger.) What you don't get is true collaboration; SharedView is more suited for computer-based dog-and-pony shows. Still, it's yet another way to share your documents and other work with colleagues over the web.

myDataBus

The myDataBus service (www.mydatabus.com) is a combination cloud storage and file-sharing service. You can use myDataBus to store your individual files or to share photos, videos, and music with your friends and family. The service also offers group collaboration tools and integration with Facebook, MySpace, LiveJournal, and other similar sites.

Nirvanix

If your storage needs are larger, consider Nirvanix (www.nirvanix.com). Nirvanix is a cloud storage platform optimized for large files and large enterprise-level customers. The Nirvanix Storage Delivery Network intelligently stores, delivers, and processes storage requests in the best network location. Storage is offered on an on-demand, completely scalable basis.

steekR

As you can see in Figure 15.2, steekR (www.steekr.com) is designed especially for consumers who want to share their documents and media files online. After you've uploaded a file, you can share it with anyone in your contact list. You can also opt to make specific files editable by other, or assign them read-only restrictions.

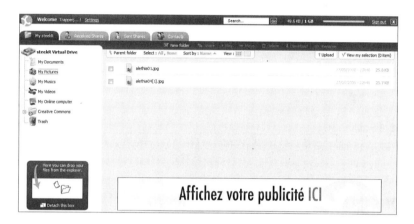

FIGURE 15.2
A cloud storage service for home users: steekR.

The basic steekR service, with 1GB of storage, is free. Paid plans, with up to 100GB of storage, are also available.

Windows Live SkyDrive

Now we come to Microsoft's second cloud storage service. Windows Live SkyDrive (skydrive.live.com) differs from Office Live Online in that you can use it to store any type of file, not just Office files. You get 5GB of free storage, and can easily share your uploaded files with others you authorize via shared or public folders. Personal folders are used for files you want to keep private.

As you can see in Figure 15.3, uploading and managing your files is accomplished via an easy-to-use graphical dashboard. Just click a folder to view its contents or open an individual file. It's quick and easy, ideal for home or

small business users—including those who want to collaborate over the web
with other users.

FIGURE 15.3
Managing your uploaded files with Windows Live SkyDrive.

Exploring Online Bookmarking Services

There's one more type of web-based data sharing service that bears discussing.
This type of service lets you share your notes and favorite websites with your
friends and colleagues—or with yourself, if you're on another computer.

It works like this. You visit a website you like and decide you want to bookmark it or share it with others. Because bookmarks and favorites work only on
a single computer, you instead save the site (and any notes you have about it)
to an online bookmarking site. This saves your bookmark and notes to the
cloud; you can then email the link to friends, or access it yourself at a later
time.

So-called notebook sites work in much the same fashion, but with random
text notes you may take on any subject. Just upload your notes to the site,
and then access them or share them via the web.

To give you an idea of what's available, let's survey just a few of the more
popular bookmarking and notebook sites.

BlinkList

BlinkList (www.blinklist.com) is an easy-to-use bookmarking site. When you sign up for the (free) service, you install a small applet in your web browser. This applet adds a Blink This Site link to your browser's favorites list. Click this link when you find a site you want to save; this displays the Blinking dialog box shown in Figure 15.4. Enter any notes you have about the site, and then click the Blink button. (You can also use this dialog box to send a link to the site to friends and family.) The site now appears on your BlinkList My List page, along with all the other sites you've "blinked."

FIGURE 15.4

"Blinking" a favorite site with BlinkList.

ClipClip

ClipClip (www.clipclip.org) does more than just bookmark favorite websites; it lets you clip and save text and images from websites and blogs to an online notebook. You can store and organize your clips for future use (great for research) or share them with others.

You clip images and text by selecting them in your web browser (using your mouse) and then clicking the ClipClip button or link. The clips are then uploaded to the ClipClip website, where you can view them yourself or share them with other users. (Figure 15.5 shows how ClipClip stores and displays the items you clip.)

FIGURE 15.5
Viewing web page clips with ClipClip.

Clipmarks

Clipmarks (www.clipmarks.com) functions much like ClipClip. You can clip any type of content from a web page and save it to the Clipmarks website. You can then access your clips at a later time from any Internet-connected computer, or share your clips with other users.

del.icio.us

The del.icio.us site is known by its unusual name, which is also its web address (del.icio.us). Shown in Figure 15.6, del.icio.us calls itself a social book-marking site, in that it lets users store and share website bookmarks. In reality, del.icio.us is perhaps the most popular of these cloud bookmarking sites, with more than 3 million users and more than 100 million bookmarked URLs. The site is now owned by Yahoo!

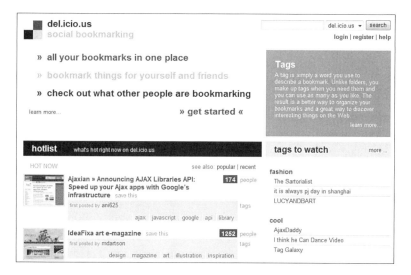

FIGURE 15.6

The most popular social bookmarking site, del.icio.us.

As with most of these sites, del.icio.us uses tags to help users find bookmarked sites. When you bookmark a site (often by clicking the del.icio.us button embedded on the site), you add a few keywords to describe the site. Other users can then search by keywords to find the most popular matching bookmarked sites.

Feedmarker

Feedmarker (www.feedmarker.com) is another bookmarking site. It's unique in that it also functions as a newsreader for RSS and Atom feeds. You can also add newsfeeds as bookmarks.

SharedCopy

SharedCopy (www.sharedcopy.com) is billed as a "collaborative annotation service." What that means is that you can save a copy of any web page to the SharedCopy site, while making all sorts of notes and highlights to that page. You can then share the annotated page with others of your choosing.

Tagseasy

Tagseasy (www.tagseasy.com) is an unusual combination of bookmarking, notebook, and cloud storage service. You can bookmark individual websites and share them with friends and colleagues, as well as upload and share individual documents (up to 1GB total storage). It's a free service, so you might want to check it out.

Yahoo! MyWeb

Yahoo! MyWeb (myweb.yahoo.com) is a simple online bookmarking service. You can easily save any bookmark to the MyWeb site, and then access it from any computer or share it with friends and colleagues.

ZOHO NOTEBOOK

Saving website URLs or clips of web page content is one way to save and organize your research. But what if you collect more than web clips—what if you also want to organize your notes, or content created in other applications?

The solution may be a cloud-based notebook, such as the one offered by Zoho Notebook (notebook.zoho.com). Zoho Notebook enables you to aggregate all types of content—text, images, audio, video, web URLs—in a single place. Your aggregated content creates a notebook, like the one in Figure 15.7.

FIGURE 15.7
Aggregating different types of content with Zoho Notebook.

You can share all or part of your notebook with other users. Sharing can be as granular as an individual page or object on a page. You can also publish all or part of your notebook to a public web page.

I like Zoho Notebook as a more holistic approach to organizing notes and information from disparate sources. It's ideal for students collecting data for reports, as well as anyone doing research of any type. The best thing is, Zoho Notebook is a web-based application, which means you can access your research from any computer, or share it with others who may be collaborating with you.

Sharing Digital Photographs

I n the preceding chapter, we discussed sites you can use to store and share all types of computer files. One particular type of file-sharing site, however, warrants coverage in its own chapter. I'm talking photo-sharing sites—those web-based sites that let you store and share your digital photographs with friends and families.

Beyond simple photo sharing, however, are sites that let you edit your digital photos. Although these sites will never equal the editing power of a high-end software program such as Adobe Photoshop CS, an online photo-editing site might be all you need to perform simple editing tasks, such as lightening or darkening a photo, cropping the frame, and so on.

So read on to learn what you can find in the cloud to help you fix and share your favorite digital photos.

Exploring Online Photo-Editing Applications

Let's start with those web-based applications you can use to edit your digital photos. After all, not every picture you take is perfect; sometimes a quick fix can turn a bad photo into an acceptable one.

What can you do with an online photo-editing program? While you don't have quite the number of options you do with most desktop photo editing software, you do get all the basics. You can crop and rotate your photos, color correct them, fix the red-eye problem, adjust contrast and brightness, and even combine multiple photos into a photo collage.

Most of these cloud applications work by having you upload your photo to the editing site first. You then make the edits you want, often by clicking a "quick fix" button of some sort. Your edited photo is then downloaded back to your computer for archiving.

Adobe Photoshop Express

The first web-based photo-editing application we'll discuss is also arguably the best. Adobe Photoshop Express (www.photoshop.com/express/) has a stellar lineage, coming from the same company that brings you Photoshop CS, the number-one photo-editing program for serious photographers. As the name implies, Photoshop Express is kind of a quick-and-dirty version of the full-featured Photoshop CS, with all the basic editing controls you need to fix the most common photo problems. Best of all, it's completely free.

You start using Photoshop Express by uploading those photos you want to edit. Your uploaded photos appear in the online library shown in Figure 16.1. To edit a photo, double-click that photo in the library.

The Photoshop Express editing window, shown in Figure 16.2, offers a variety of different editing options, grouped as follows:

- **Basics**. Crop, rotate, auto correct, exposure, red-eye removal, touchup (a blur effect to remove scratches and blemishes), and color saturation control
- **Tuning**. White balance, highlight, fill light, sharpen, and soft focus
- **Effects**. Pop color, change hue, black & white, tint, sketch, and distort

This is far and away the largest collection of editing and enhancement options of any online photo editor. Suffice to say, just about anything that's wrong with a photo, you can fix online with Photoshop Express.

FIGURE 16.1

Uploaded images in the Photoshop Express online library.

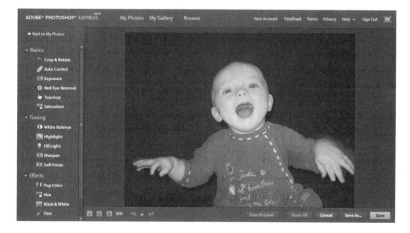

FIGURE 16.2

Editing an image with Photoshop Express.

Adobe lets you store up to 2GB of photos. And, like many other web-based photo editors, Photoshop Express is integrated with Flickr, so you can upload your edited photos to the Flickr site with a minimum of fuss and muss.

FotoFlexer

FotoFlexer (www.fotoflexer.com), like Photoshop Express, is completely free to use. It offers similar editing options as Photoshop Express, with even more interesting enhancement tools.

As you can see in Figure 16.3, the FotoFlexer editing window displays your currently uploaded photo in a tabbed interface. Each tab is designed for a particular editing/enhancement task, with its own row of option buttons along the top. For example, the Basic tab includes buttons for Auto Fix, Fix Red Eye, Crop, Resize, Rotate, Flip, Adjust (hue, saturation, and lightness), and Contrast. Other tabs let you apply special effects, decorations, animations, and distortions. The Layers tab even lets you use multiple layers for editing and effects.

FIGURE 16.3

FotoFlexer's Basic editing tab.

Picnik

Picnik (www.picnik.com) is one of the easier-to-use web-based photo-editing applications. As you can see in Figure 16.4, the editing functions include the basics: auto-fix, rotate, crop, resize, exposure, colors, sharpen, and red-eye removal. Click any button to display the control for that particular option.

You can also apply a variety of special effects by clicking the Create tab. Here you can apply effects like black and white, sepia, night vision, pencil sketch, film grain, and the like. Just click a button to apply a given effect.

FIGURE 16.4

The basic editing functions in Picnik.

Picture2Life

As you can see in Figure 16.5, Picture2Life (www.picture2life.com) offers a combination of basic editing and special effects. The basic editing options include crop, resize, and rotate, as well as adjustments for brightness, contrast, color, and the like. The special effects include edge fades, Gaussian blur, emboss, pixelate, and the like. In addition, Picture2Life lets you create collages and animated GIF files from your photos.

FIGURE 16.5

Editing a photo with Picture2Life.

Pikifx

Pikifx (www.pikifx.com) is perhaps the simplest and easiest-to-use online photo editor I've found. As you can see in Figure 16.6, you have some very basic options at the top of the page; you can resize or crop your photo, or add borders, text, or various special effects. Applying an effect is as easy as clicking the thumbnail for that effect; there are no sliders or controls to adjust.

FIGURE 16.6

Applying effects with Pikifx.

Preloadr

Preloadr (www.preloadr.com) is interesting for two reasons. First, it's tightly integrated with Flickr. In fact, you have to log in to your Flickr account to access the Preloadr editor. Second, Preloadr offers a variety of professional editing tools not found on other editing sites, such as layers, curves, histograms, and the like.

After you log in, you're shown a list of all the photos you've previously uploaded to Flickr. You can then edit any of these photos, using either the basic interface or the advanced tools shown in Figure 16.7. After you've editing a photo, you can then replace the previous version on Flickr with the newly edited version.

FIGURE 16.7

Using Preloadr's advanced editing tools.

Phixr

Phixr (www.phixr.com) is a free online photo editor with basic editing functions. As you can see in Figure 16.8, Phixr's editing interface resembles that of Photoshop and other popular photo-editing programs; the basic editing options are available via the buttons to the left of the main picture.

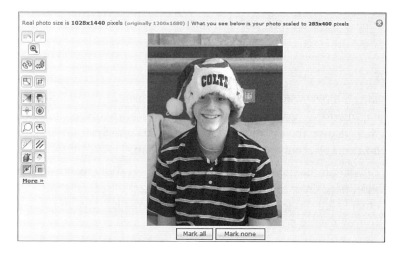

FIGURE 16.8

Phixr's Photoshop-like editing interface.

Phixr lets you rotate, crop, or flip a photo. You can also adjust color, make the photo black and white or sepia tone, add text or cartoon bubbles, and apply a variety of special effects.

Pixenate

Pixenate (www.pixenate.com) also offers a button-oriented editing interface. As you can see in Figure 16.9, you apply an effect by clicking the button to the left of the picture. Just the Undo button if you don't like the results.

FIGURE 16.9
Click a button to apply an effect with Pixenate.

Snipshot

Snipshot (www.snipshot.com), formerly known as Pixoh, offers a snazzy editing interface. As you can see in Figure 16.10, when you click a button above your picture, the associated control appears onscreen. Click the Effects button, for example, and the Effects control pops up.

You get all the basic editing controls (tint, exposure, contrast, saturation, hue, sharpness, crop, and resize) as well as a bevy of special effects. Unlike some other cloud services, Snipshot lets you edit really large images—up to 10MB in size, or 5000 x 5000 pixels.

FIGURE 16.10

Snazzy photo editing with Snipshot.

Exploring Photo-Sharing Communities

Editing your photos with a web-based application is convenient; you can do your editing from any computer, no software installation necessary. Even more convenient is the ability to share your photos with others through the cloud, via web-based photo-sharing communities.

On the surface, all of these photo-sharing sites look and feel quite similar. You choose your photos to upload, organize them in albums or folders, and select whether they're private or public. Some sites let your friends download your photos; others only allow online viewing. Some sites even let you or your friends make prints of your photos—for a fee, of course. And the most robust sites include topic-oriented groups and communities that let you share photos with like-minded photographers.

note Most of these sites offer some sort of free membership, which sometimes has limited functionality. Some sites offer paid memberships with more advanced features. Other sites make their money by offering photo-printing services.

Apple MobileMe Gallery

One interesting part of Apple's new MobileMe suite of web-based applications is the MobileMe Gallery (www.me.com). You can upload photos from your computer or iPhone to the MobileMe Gallery, which can then be viewed by anyone you invite. It's a great way to get photos on and off your iPhone, and view photos when you're on the go.

Figure 16.11 shows how MobileMe Gallery organizes your photos into easy-to-view photo albums. The entire MobileMe suite is priced at $99 per year, and includes 20GB of total storage.

FIGURE 16.11
Online photo albums in Apple's MobileMe Gallery.

dotPhoto

The dotPhoto site (www.dotphoto.com) is free for personal users, but there's a heavy push to order photo prints. Professional photographers can use dotPhoto to house photos displayed on their own websites—and collect a cut when users order prints.

DPHOTO

DPHOTO (www.dphoto.com) offers two levels of membership. The Lite version lets you store up to 1,000 photos for $3/month; the Pro version offers unlimited photo storage for $7/month. Like many of these sites, DPHOTO assigns you your own personal web address for your photos, in the form of *yourname*.dphoto.com.

Flickr

Of all the photo-sharing sites today, far and away the most popular among hobbyist and professional photographers is Flickr (www.flickr.com), part of the Yahoo! empire. As you can see in Figure 16.12, Flickr creates a home page for each photographer. From here, viewers can click a photo to view it full screen, or choose to view all photos as an onscreen slideshow.

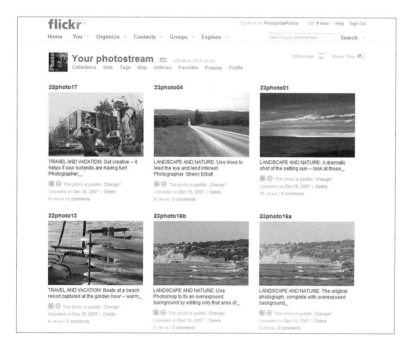

FIGURE 16.12

A typical Flickr user page.

Uploading photos to Flickr is as easy as clicking a few links (after you've opened your free account, of course). Just go to Flickr's home page and click the Upload Photos link. You're then prompted to choose the files to upload and add tags and descriptions to each photo. The photos you upload are then added to your personal page for anyone (or selected users, if you made the photos private) to view.

Flickr's free accounts let you upload 100MB of photos each month. If you need to upload more photos, or want more control over how your photos are displayed, consider paying for a Pro account. For $24.95/year, you get unlimited uploads and storage, as well as the ability to organize your photos into sets and collections.

> **note** Learn more about Flickr and digital photography in general in my companion book, *Photopedia: The Ultimate Digital Photography Reference*. You can view many of the photos from that book on Flickr, at www.flickr.com/photos/12150723@N06/.

One of the best things about Flickr is the site's community, expressed via comments on particular photos and a large number of topic-specific photo groups. The groups not only display photos from group members but also include discussion forums where members can talk about the topic at hand. If you're at all interested in photography as a hobby or profession, Flickr is the site to use.

Fotki

Fotki (www.fotki.com), like Flickr, offers both free and paid accounts. A free account gives you 50MB of storage space, and the $30/year premium account has unlimited storage and a variety of other features, including the ability to sell your photos from the Fotki site.

MyPhotoAlbum

MyPhotoAlbum (www.myphotoalbum.com), as the site's name implies, focuses on displaying your digital photos in online photo albums. You get a unique web address for your album, which makes it easy to share your album with friends and family. You can even personalize your album with custom themes and layouts. And, best of all, it's all free.

Photobucket

Photobucket (www.photobucket.com) is another free photo-sharing site. You can create photo albums for viewing on the Photobucket site or embed your Photobucket photos into your blog or Facebook or MySpace page.

Picasa Web Albums

Picasa Web Albums (picasaweb.google.com) is Google's entrée into the photo-sharing market. As you might suspect, Picasa Web Albums is closely integrated with Google's Picasa photo-editing software, although it's open for anyone to use—and it's free. There's also a neat mapping option that lets you map where you took each photo, using Google Maps.

Pixagogo

Pixagogo (www.pixagogo.com) costs $5/month to use. For that, you can upload and store an unlimited number of photos. You also get your own personal photo gallery. For what it's worth, the site also pushes hard on ordering prints, so keep that in mind when you're doing your evaluating.

PictureTrail

PictureTrail (www.picturetrail.com) offers photo sharing, fancy online slideshows, and a photo editor that lets you add "bling," in the form of fancy graphics, to your photos. Membership is free.

SmugMug

SmugMug (www.smugmug.com) is a photo-sharing community that aims to compete directly with Flickr. As such, SmugMug offers a slightly better-looking interface and unlimited storage, for $39.95/year. And, remembering the advantages of cloud storage, SmugMug keeps three copies of your photos on servers housed in four different states, for more secure photo storage.

WebShots

WebShots (www.webshots.com) is an established photo-sharing community with many Flickr-like features. The free account lets you upload 1,000 photos (plus 100 more for each month of membership); the premium account lets you share 5,000 photos (plus 500 more for each month of membership) for $2.49/month.

Zenfolio

Zenfolio (www.zenfolio.com) is designed as a place for professional photographers to store, show, and sell their work. The site offers three different hosting plans: Basic (1GB storage for $25/year), Unlimited (unlimited storage for $40/year), and Premium (unlimited storage and larger file sizes for $100/year).

Zoto

Our final photo-sharing site is Zoto (www.zoto.com), which offers unlimited storage for $19.95/year. Zoto lets users store and share photos on the Zoto site, in a variety of photo albums. You can also publish your Zoto photos to your blog or Flickr account.

COMMERCIAL PHOTO-PRINTING/SHARING SERVICES

The photo-sharing sites we've discussed so far in this chapter are independent sites with a focus on storage and sharing. Even though some of them offer photo prints as a service, their main purpose is to store your photos on their own cloud servers.

There is another class of photo-storage/sharing sites, however. While these sites do store your photos, they exist to make money—by selling photo prints to you and your friends. These photo-print sites, such as Shutterfly (www.shutterfly.com) and Hewlett-Packard's Snapfish (www.snapfish.com), offer many of the same sharing features as Flickr and WebShots, but typically without the community features. Storage is often unlimited and free, with the hope that you'll be ordering lots of prints.

Of course, you can also order prints online from companies such as Wal-Mart, Walgreens, CVS Pharmacy, Costco, and the like. These sites let you order prints via mail or pick them up at your local store. For that matter, Shutterfly, in addition to its prints-by-mail service, lets you pick up certain-sized prints at your local Target store. It's all in the service of selling prints, of course; the online storage and sharing is just a convenient by-product.

Controlling It All with Web-Based Desktops

In the previous chapters in this section, we discussed all manner of cloud services, from web-based calendars and contact management applications to online word processors, spreadsheets, and presentation programs. But there's one more category of application that's worth examining—one that ties all these applications together into a single browser window.

This type of application isn't an application at all; it's actually a mini operating system that replicates the basic features of Windows or the Mac OS, plus key productivity applications, in a single cloud service. We're talking about something called a web-based desktop; and if you're serious about moving your computing into the cloud, this may be the way to go.

Understanding Web-Based Desktops

A web-based desktop, or *webtop*, is essentially a virtual computer desktop displayed inside your web browser, delivered over any Internet connection. A web desktop has

a graphical user interface (GUI) like Windows or the Mac OS, and often comes complete with one or more productivity applications. The webtop and all its apps, as well as your personal preferences for how the desktop looks, are stored in the cloud, and you access it over the web.

What kind of apps come with a typical webtop? In almost all cases, it includes basics such as a web browser, email program (for the hosting site's web-based email service), web calendar, and maybe even instant messaging client. In many instances, the application suite also includes a word processor and spreadsheet, and maybe even a presentation program. In other words, all the apps you need to be functional in the office or on the road are included.

Of course, the chief benefit of a web-based desktop is that you get your own personalized computing environment that follows you around from computer to computer—or even to compatible cell phones and handhelds. All you have to do is log on to your desktop from any web browser, and everything you do—all your apps and files—is right there, same as it was the last you left them. And it's all completely personalized with the colors, backgrounds, and order you specify.

Interestingly, some people refer to web-based desktops as web-based operating systems, because they deliver OS-like functionality over the web. I don't buy that, because a webtop does not replace your current operating system; it sits on top of it—or, more accurately, inside your web browser.

That said, many web-based desktops look and feel a lot like your favorite operating system. Some mimic Windows right down to the taskbar and Start button. Others do their best *not* to look like Windows, figuring you've had enough of that. Naturally, you should pick the webtop that looks and feels most natural to you.

Evaluating Web-Based Desktops

There are a number of competing web-based desktops. Some are free, some are subscription based. We'll look at the most popular in alphabetic order.

ajaxWindows

One of the most fully developed web desktops is ajaxWindows (www.ajaxwindows.com). This webtop integrates several key applications, including ajaxWrite, ajaxSketch, and ajaxPresent.

As you can see in Figure 17.1, the ajaxWindows interface is very Windows-like, which should make it easy for beginners to get comfortable with. The desktop duplicates much of the functionality of the standard Windows desktop, including desktop icons, a start menu, taskbar, and Sidebar-like widgets. Of course, you can add your own programs as icons to the desktop and customize the desktop's background and color scheme.

FIGURE 17.1
The Windows-like virtual desktop of ajaxWindows.

Although you have to sign up to get full functionality (with online storage thanks to Gmail), registration is free. The wide range of apps plus the free cost makes ajaxWindows a good choice for all users.

Deskjump

Deskjump (www.deskjump.com) offers a variety of easy-to-use applications housed on a common desktop, as shown in Figure 17.2. You get a simple word processor, spreadsheet, email client, address book, online calendar, picture viewer, and file manager, as well as 1GB online storage space and your own blog and website. Although Deskjump doesn't offer the most sophisticated applications, it is free and easy to use.

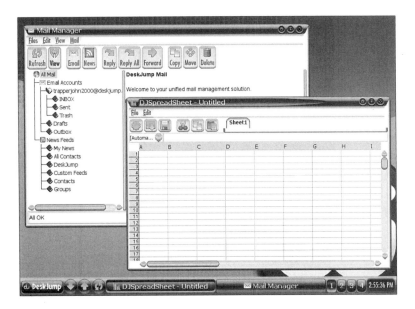

FIGURE 17.2
The web-based desktop and basic applications of Deskjump.

Desktoptwo

Desktoptwo (www.desktoptwo.com) offers a relatively uncluttered desktop, as you can see in Figure 17.3, except for an annoying ad window that just won't go away. (That's how they get away with their free service, I suppose.) The apps included aren't as plentiful as with some other desktops; there's email, a calendar, an address book, instant messaging, an MP3 player, and a notepad—but no word processor or spreadsheet.

eyeOS

The eyeOS (www.eyeos.org) offers a suite of useful applications, including a word processor, spreadsheet, presentation program, email client, contact manager, calendar, photo viewer, and file manager. All apps are compatible with Microsoft Office file formats. As you can see in Figure 17.4, the desktop is very simple, with a task-based "start" panel helping new users get started.

FIGURE 17.3

Desktoptwo—complete with annoying advertising window.

FIGURE 17.4

The clean eyeOS desktop—complete with "start" panel.

g.ho.st

The initials stand for "globally hosted operating system," which is exactly what g.ho.st is. (And the URL mirrors the name—yes, it's actually g.ho.st.) You get 5GB of online file storage, FTP access, instant messaging, a web browser, and an email client. Productivity apps are courtesy of Zoho and include Zoho Writer and Zoho Sheets. You also get a bevy of desktop widgets, as shown in Figure 17.5—enough to feel cluttered, at least until you personalize your own desktop.

FIGURE 17.5

The cluttered g.ho.st desktop, complete with multiple widgets.

Glide

We've discussed Glide's various web-based applications elsewhere in this book; combine them all into a single desktop and you get the Glide OS (www.glidedigital.com). The Glide OS, shown in Figure 17.6, includes a word processor (Write), spreadsheet (Crunch), presentation program (Present), photo editor, calendar, email client, media player, virtual online hard drive, and more.

Nivio

The Nivio (www.nivio.com) desktop should be familiar to most computer users; as you can see in Figure 17.7, it's essentially Windows 2000, hosted on the web and piped into your web browser. For $4.99/month you get Nivio's web-based version of Windows 2000, complete with Microsoft Office (including Word, Excel, and PowerPoint), Microsoft Explorer, Adobe Reader, and other popular applications. This makes Nivio perhaps the most full featured of all web-based desktops—certainly the one with the most familiar productivity applications.

FIGURE 17.6

The feature-rich desktop of the Glide OS.

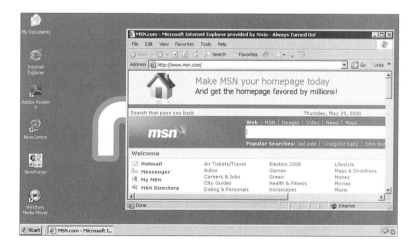

FIGURE 17.7

Nivio—Windows 2000 in the cloud.

StartForce

StartForce (www.startforce.com) provides a Windows-like desktop, complete with green Start button for the start menu, as you can see in Figure 17.8. The desktop is integrated with Zoho's web-based productivity applications, and also comes with an instant messaging client, web browser, and media player. Also included is a file loader for bulk uploading.

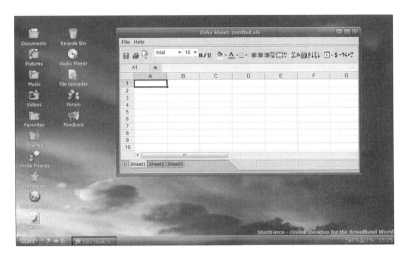

FIGURE 17.8

The StartForce desktop, complete with Zoho applications.

YouOS

Our final web-based desktop is YouOS (www.youos.com), which is a simpler desktop than some of the others discussed here. As you can see in Figure 17.9, the desktop contains a simple text editor, file manager, web browser, chat/instant messaging client, and sticky note app. Not a lot of customization is possible. For what it's worth, the company bills YouOS as an "application community," where developers can create their own YouOS apps or widgets.

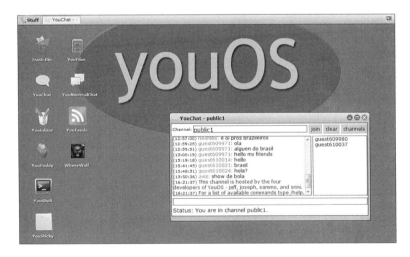

FIGURE 17.9

The relatively simple YouOS desktop.

ALMOST A DESKTOP: APPLE'S MOBILEME

Throughout this book we've discussed several companies that offer entire suites of web-based applications, the most notable being Google and Zoho. While these companies don't offer complete web-based desktops, you can put their apps together into what amounts to a virtual desktop of your own making.

As of mid-2008, Google and Zoho have a new competitor in this web-based suite space, in the form of Apple MobileMe. MobileMe is Apple's foray into cloud computing, with a variety of useful applications hosted on Apple's cloud.

MobileMe includes the following applications:

- Mail (email)
- Contacts (contact management)
- Calendar (calendar and scheduling)
- Gallery (photo gallery and sharing)
- iDisk (online file storage)

One of the unique things about MobileMe is that it isn't limited to just PC (Windows or Mac) access; you can also access your MobileMe apps and documents via Apple's iPhone or iPod touch. That makes MobileMe the ultimate in on-the-go application suites, accessible virtually anywhere you have a Wi-Fi or cell phone signal.

MobileMe is as snazzy as you'd expect from Apple, which should appeal to trendy users everywhere. While Google and Zoho offer their equivalent web-based apps for free, Apple charges $99/year for a single-user MobileMe subscription, or $149 for a five-user "family pack." For that you get access to all the MobileMe applications plus 20GB online storage (40GB for the family pack). That makes MobileMe one of the pricier cloud offerings available today—although if anyone can command the price, Apple probably can.

You can learn more about Apple's Mobile Me at www.me.com, which is a pretty cool URL, if nothing else. If you're serious about cloud services, and especially if you're an iPhone user, it's worth checking out.

Outside the Cloud: Other Ways to Collaborate Online

Collaborating via Web-Based Communication Tools

In this final section of the book, we go beyond cloud storage and services into cloud-related communication tools. Although not all of these tools are strictly cloud based (some use the host's proprietary servers in a traditional client/server relationship, others are peer to peer in nature), they are all web based and all serve to further group collaboration—two of the core tenants of cloud computing.

What kinds of communication tools are we talking about? There are three main categories: web email services, instant messaging services, and web conferencing tools. Groups located anywhere in the world can use these tools to communicate with other group members—and further their collaboration on group projects.

Evaluating Web Mail Services

Traditional email is anything but cloud based. The type of email program you probably have installed on your PC uses a protocol called the Post Office Protocol (POP). POP email requires the use of a dedicated email *client* program, such as Microsoft Outlook or Outlook Express, and—at the ISP level— email servers to send and receive messages.

The problem with traditional POP email is that you're tied to the client program installed on your PC. The messages you receive are stored on that PC, and you usually can't access them when you're traveling or away from that PC. There are none of the "anytime, anywhere" advantages you're used to with cloud-based services.

Fortunately, there is a better way to manage your email—in the form of web-based email services, also known as web mail or HTTP email. Unlike traditional POP email, web mail can be accessed from any PC using any web browser, and all your messages are stored on the web, not locally. It's just like a cloud service; no special software required. This lets you retrieve and manage your email when you're out of the office or on the road.

Not only is web mail more versatile than traditional POP email, it's also easier to set up. All you need to know is your user ID and password, and then you access a page that lets you view the contents of your inbox, read and reply to messages, create new messages, and (in many cases) store messages in folders. You can even, on some services, use your web mail account to access your ISP's POP email.

The three largest web mail services today are hosted by Google, Microsoft, and Yahoo! In addition, most of the web desktops we discussed in Chapter 17, "Controlling It All with Web-Based Desktops," also have their own web mail services. So you have plenty of choices when it comes to sending and receiving email via the web.

Gmail

Google's web mail service is called Gmail (mail.google.com), and at first blush it looks a lot like the other services we discuss in this chapter. Gmail is free, it lets you send and receive email from any web browser, and the interface even looks similar to its competitors, as you can see in Figure 18.1.

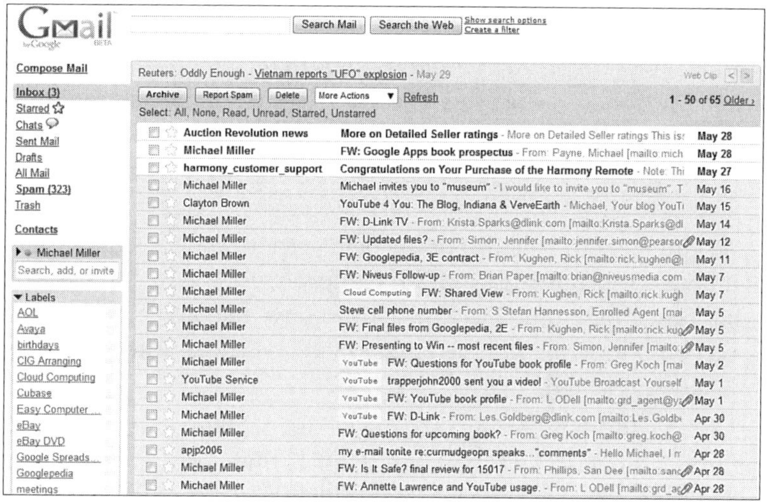

FIGURE 18.1

The Gmail inbox.

But Gmail offers a few unique features that set it apart from the web-based email crowd. First, Gmail doesn't use folders. That's right, with Gmail you can't organize your mail into folders, as you can with the other services. Instead, Gmail pushes the search paradigm as the way to find the messages you want—not a surprise, given Google's search-centric business model.

Gmail does, however, let you "tag" each message with one or more labels. This has the effect of creating virtual folders, as you can search and sort your messages by any of their labels.

In addition, Gmail groups together related email messages in what Google calls *conversations*. A conversation might be an initial message and all the replies (and replies to replies) to that message; a conversation might also be all the daily emails from a single source that have a common subject, such as messages from subscribed-to mailing lists.

Like most of the other services we discuss here, Gmail is a free service; all you have to do is sign up for an account. Of course, if you already have an account for any other Google service, that account can serve as your Gmail account. When you sign up for your Gmail account, you get assigned your email address (in the form of *name*@gmail.com) and you get access to the Gmail inbox page. As of June 2008, Gmail offered 6GB of storage for users.

Yahoo! Mail

Yahoo! Mail (mail.yahoo.com) is another web mail service, provided by the popular Yahoo! search site. The basic Yahoo! Mail is free and can be accessed from any PC, using any web browser. Yahoo! also offers a paid service called Yahoo! Mail Plus that lets you send larger messages and offers offline access to your messages via POP email clients.

Whether you use the free or the paid version, Yahoo! Mail gives you unlimited storage—which means you can effectively use Yahoo! Mail as an online backup or file-storage system. All you have to do is email yourself those files you want to store, and then place those messages (with attachments) in your designated storage folder.

As you can see in Figure 18.2, the Yahoo! Mail interface is more functional than that offered by Gmail. It also offers traditional folder-based organization. You get a message pane and a reading pane, just as you do with Microsoft Outlook. Yahoo! also offers users the SpamGuard spam filter and Norton AntiVirus virus scanner.

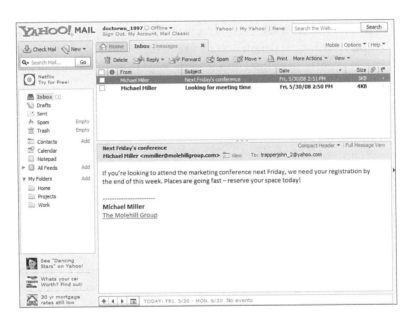

FIGURE 18.2
Previewing messages with Yahoo! Mail.

Windows Live Hotmail

Hotmail was one of the first web-based email services, and it's still one of the largest. But it's not called "Hotmail" anymore; Microsoft has moved it into its Windows Live suite of online services and now calls it Windows Live Hotmail.

note Hotmail started life (in 1996) as an independent company, but was acquired by software behemoth Microsoft in 1997.

Like most web mail services, Hotmail (we're going to call it by its old, shorter name) can be accessed from any web browser on any PC anywhere in the world, for free. Microsoft gives you 5GB of storage, not quite as much as you get with Gmail (6GB) or Yahoo! Mail (unlimited).

As you can see in Figure 18.3, the new Windows Live Hotmail interface is as snazzy as they come. You have your folder pane on the left, message page in the middle, and reading pane on the right. The new Hotmail also integrates with your Windows Live contacts and calendar, as well as other Windows Live services.

FIGURE 18.3
The new Windows Live Hotmail interface.

Apple MobileMe Mail

As part of its MobileMe suite of applications, Apple offers MobileMe Mail (www.me.com). What makes MobileMe Mail unique is that it's not limited to just computer users; you can also send and receive emails from your Apple iPhone or iPod touch, via Wi-Fi Internet or cellular network.

MobileMe Mail is a web-based service that can also be accessed with your existing Mac or Windows-based email program, including Outlook, Outlook Express, and Windows Mail. It has its own native interface on the iPhone and iPod touch, as shown in Figure 18.4.

FIGURE 18.4
MobileMe Mail on an Apple iPhone.

Unlike the other webmail services discussed here, MobileMe Mail isn't free. It's part of the MobileMe suite of applications, which costs $99 per year. (But you do get a really cool .me email address!)

OtherWeb Mail Services

Gmail, Yahoo! Mail, and Windows Live Hotmail are the three largest web mail services (and MobileMe Mail promises to be a competitor), but there are literally hundreds more. Besides these big providers, there are dozens of independent web mail services, plus a plethora of topic-specific websites that offer (among other content and services) their own branded HTTP email. In addition, just about every cloud service provider, such as Zoho, offers web mail as part of its suite; web mail is also part of most web-based desktops.

So if you're looking for a web mail service and don't want to go with one of the big three, here's a short list of some of the other major providers to check out:

- AOL Mail (mail.aol.com)
- BigString (www.bigstring.com)
- Excite Mail (mail.excite.com)
- FlashMail (www.flashmail.com)
- GMX Mail (www.gmx.com)
- Inbox.com (www.inbox.com)
- Lycos Mail (mail.lycos.com)
- Mail.com (www.mail.com)
- Zoho Mail (zoho.mail.com)

Evaluating Instant Messaging Services

Email is just one way to communicate online. For many users, instant messaging is a better way to talk; it's more immediate, because you can send text messages in real time to your friends and coworkers. No more waiting for people to respond to your emails—when both parties are online at the same time, it's just like having a one-on-one conversation!

Technology-wise, email works a little differently from most Internet applications—and quite different from the cloud services we've been discussing throughout this book. Email (both web based and POP), Usenet, and the World Wide Web operate via a traditional client/server model, with most of the heavy lifting done via a network of dedicated servers. For example, your POP email is stored on and managed by an email server, while all the pages on the web are hosted on millions of individual web servers.

Instant messaging, however, doesn't use servers at all. When you send an instant message to another user, that message goes directly to that user's PC; it's not filtered by or stored on any servers. The technical name for this type of connection is *peer-to-peer* (P2P), because the two computers involved are peers to each other.

All instant messaging needs to work is a piece of client software (one for each computer involved, of course) and the IP addresses of each computer. The messages go directly from one IP address to another, with no servers in the middle to slow things down. (Naturally, the data must still make its way through numerous routers to get to the other PC, but that's part and parcel of any Internet-based application.)

There are several big players in the instant messaging market today, including America Online (with both AOL Instant Messenger and ICQ), Google (Google Talk), Microsoft (Windows Live Messenger), and Yahoo! (Yahoo! Messenger). Unfortunately, most of these products don't work well (or at all) with each other. If you're using Yahoo! Messenger, for example, you can't communicate with someone running AOL Instant Messenger. That means you'll want to use the IM program that all your friends and coworkers are using—so find that out before you download any software.

AOL Instant Messenger

The most-used instant messaging program is AOL Instant Messenger (www.aim.com), also known as AIM. AOL claims more than 60 million users, which makes it the number-two IM service today, second only to Yahoo! Messenger. For whatever reason, AIM is especially popular among the teen and preteen crowd, although people of all ages can and do use it.

AIM, shown in Figure 18.5, supports all manner of special features in addition to basic text messaging. You get file sharing, RSS feeds, group chats, ability to text message to and from mobile phones, voice chat, video chat, and even a mobile client. You can also enhance the basic AIM experience with a variety of official and user-created plug-ins.

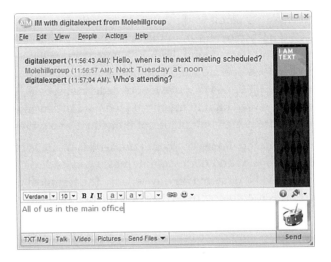

FIGURE 18.5

Communicating with AOL Instant Messenger (AIM).

Google Talk

Google Talk is the name of both Google's instant messaging network and its IM client. You can download the Google Talk client and learn more about the Google Talk network at talk.google.com.

You can access Google Talk from a web-based Google Talk gadget, a stand-alone Google Talk client program (similar to what's offered by both AIM and Yahoo! Messenger), or from your Gmail and iGoogle web pages. As with competing IM systems, Google Talk lets you send and receive both text-based instant messages and Voice over IP (VoIP) Internet phone calls.

Most people will use Google Talk via the web-based Google Talk "gadget." You launch the Google Talk gadget by going to talk.google.com and clicking the Launch Google Talk button. With the gadget, there's no software to download; Google Talk opens in its own small browser window, as shown in Figure 18.6.

FIGURE 18.6

Instant messaging with the web-based Google Talk gadget.

If you want increased functionality, such as file transfer, you can download the Google Talk *client*, which is a separate software program. The main Google Talk client window looks a lot like the Google Talk gadget window; however, if the person you're chatting with also has the Google Talk client installed, you can send files back and forth between yourselves, using the Send Files button.

> **note** Google Talk has recently been connected to the AOL Instant Messenger network—so you can now use Google Talk to message with all your AIM buddies, and vice versa.

Unfortunately, Google Talk isn't as widely used as competing IM services. I'm not sure why that is, but you'll definitely want to make sure your friends or coworkers are using Google Talk before you settle on this service for your IM needs.

> **note** ICQ stands for "I seek you"—say it out loud.

ICQ

The granddaddy of all instant messaging programs is ICQ (www.icq.com). ICQ was birthed by a company named Mirabilis back in 1996, but was acquired by America Online in 1998. Today, AOL maintains ICQ and AIM as separate programs—so separate that ICQ users can't talk to AIM users, or vice versa.

Like most other IM programs, ICQ is totally free. You also get grouped conversations, voice messaging, photo viewing, and other state-of-the-art features.

Windows Live Messenger

Not surprisingly, Microsoft is a major participant in the instant messaging market. The program currently known as Windows Live Messenger does all the main things AIM and Yahoo! Messenger do, including voice chat and the ability to page a contact's mobile phone. With more than 27 million users, Windows Live Messenger is a solid middle-of-the-pack player.

> **note** Windows Live Messenger was formally known as both MSN Messenger and Windows Messenger.

Yahoo! Messenger

With more than 90 million users, the most popular instant messenger program today is Yahoo! Messenger, shown in Figure 18.7. In addition to traditional text messaging, Yahoo! Messenger features voice and video messaging, PC-to-phone and PC-to-PC calling, voicemail, file sharing, and chat rooms. It also lets you receive up-to-the-minute stock prices, news headlines, sports scores, weather forecasts, and notification of any waiting Yahoo! Mail—all courtesy of the Yahoo! family of services.

note Many of the companies that offer web-based productivity applications also offer some form of proprietary instant messaging or chat service; so do most of the web-based desktops. These services, such as Zoho Chat (chat.zoho.com) set up private IM networks between registered users; they don't work with the major instant messaging services. To that end, these proprietary services are useful for team members collaborating on a project—assuming they're all using the company's other cloud services—but not for general IM purposes.

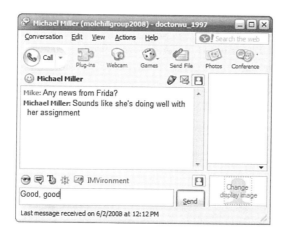

FIGURE 18.7

Yahoo! Messenger—the most popular instant messaging service today.

Evaluating Web Conferencing Tools

Email is great for one-one-one communications that aren't time sensitive. Instant messaging is better for time-sensitive communications, but it's still essentially a one-on-one medium.

When you need to include more than two people in your communications, or when you want to give a presentation to a group of people who aren't all in the same location, a different communications tool is needed. This new tool is called a *web conference*, and it's a way to conduct live meetings and presentations over the Internet.

In a typical web conference, each participant sits at his own computer in his own location. Each participant's computer is connected to the conference via the Internet, and each participant sees the presentation on his or her screen, in real time.

A web conference can be one way, as when the presenter delivers some sort of PowerPoint-like presentation, or two way, where each participant can join in and show the contents of their active applications or desktops. Communication between participants can be audio only (via streaming audio, VoIP, or traditional telephony) or include audio and video (typically using webcams).

Most web conferencing services are hosted on the vendor's servers. You typically have to arrange a conference in advance, and the hosting service will help you set everything up. Depending on the vendor, this can be a costly service, viable only for larger organizations. Make sure you check the price before you commit to using a particular service.

What features can you expect from a web conferencing service? Here are some of the most common:

- **Application sharing**, where the presenter and participants can all access and use the same application in real time. This is useful for smaller group meetings, when all participants are collaborating on a project.
- **Desktop sharing**, similar to application sharing, but with the presenter's entire desktop visible and accessible to participants.
- **File and document sharing**, with individual files and documents open for all to edit, also useful for group collaboration.
- **PowerPoint presentations**, the core component of large presentations; the presenter gives a PowerPoint presentation in real time, complete with slide transitions and animations, using audio conferencing tools to narrate the presentation.

- **Presenter notes**, which let the presenter take notes during the course of the conference for future action.

- **Annotation**, which lets the presenter mark up the document or presentation being shared or given, typically by drawing or highlighting on the screen.

- **Whiteboard**, which is a blank screen on which the presenter or participants can draw or highlight objects.

- **Text-based chat**, which lets participants discuss the presentation with each other in real time.

- **Audio conferencing**, which adds the spoken words of the presenter to a PowerPoint presentation. With two-way audio, all participants can speak—assuming that they all have microphones, of course.

- **Video conferencing**, which puts a picture of the presenter in a corner of the conference webtop, typically generated via webcam. With two-way video, conference participants can also show pictures of themselves onscreen.

- **Polling**, which lets the presenter ask questions of the audience.

- **Quizzes**, which lets participants answer test questions, typically with results tabulated in real time.

Some web conferencing systems will have all of these features; others will have a subset. Look for services that offer those features essential to your particular needs.

Adobe Acrobat Connect

The Adobe Acrobat Connect (www.adobe.com/products/acrobatconnect) software and service offers personal online "meeting rooms" for large organizations. For $39/month (and up), you get audio/video conferencing, screen sharing, whiteboard, and chat functionality.

Figure 18.8 shows a typical web conference using Acrobat connect. The main window is the shared application—that is, the live desktop of the presenter. The presenter appears via webcam in the upper-left window, and individual text chats can take place in the window below.

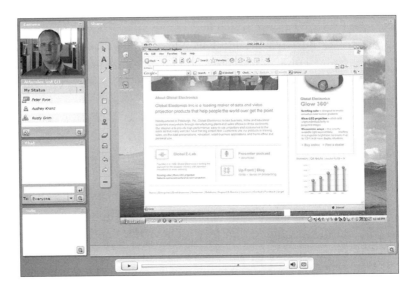

FIGURE 18.8
An Adobe Acrobat Connect web conference.

Convenos Meeting Center

The Convenos Meeting Center (www.convenos.com) is a web-based conferencing service that starts at $30/month. For that price, you get online presentations, file and document sharing, whiteboard, polling (the ability to ask questions of your audience), and integration with Skype for conference audio.

Genesys Meeting Center

The similarly named Genesys Meeting Center (www.genesys.com) offers similar features to that of the Convenos service. Genesys gives you online PowerPoint presentations, file and document sharing, chat, desktop video, whiteboard, and polling and E-Quizzes. Pricing is by request only.

Glance

Glance (www.glance.net) is a web-based conferencing service priced from $49.95/month. Its main focus is easy-to-use screen sharing, with no client software necessary to install.

IBM Lotus Sametime

IBM's web conferencing service is dubbed Lotus Sametime (www.ibm.com/sametime/), and it comes in several different versions: Entry, Standard, Advanced, and Unyte. The web conferencing service comes complete with enterprise instant messaging, multiway chat, VoIP and point-to-point video, and integration with most major desktop applications. Pricing varies by size of company.

> **note** Microsoft also offers the Office Communications Server, which enables large enterprises to host their own web conferences and instant messaging.

Microsoft Office Live Meeting

Microsoft Office Live Meeting (office.microsoft.com/en-us/livemeeting/) is a hosted service available in two versions (Standard and Professional). You get audio/video conferences, a PowerPoint viewer, integration with Microsoft Outlook, application and desktop sharing, and the like. Pricing is on a per-user basis, with volume licensing available.

Persony Web Conferencing

Unlike most other services, Persony Web Conferencing (www.persony.com) doesn't charge a monthly fee. Instead, you pay once for the software (a hefty $995) and don't have any usage fees. This means, of course, that Persony doesn't host your web conferences; you need to host conferences on your company's own servers. You get screen sharing, presentation sharing, whiteboard, picture sharing, VoIP audio, file transfer, and chat messaging.

Pixion PictureTalk

Pixion's PictureTalk (www.pixion.com) is a hosted conference solution with four different plans. The Per Minute plan charges you only for time used; the Personal plan charges you for a single 10-person virtual meeting room; the Professional Plan is priced by the seat; and the Enterprise plan lets you host the whole shebang on your own servers. All plans feature application and desktop sharing, whiteboard, polling and quizzes, chat and VoIP, audio conferencing, and the like.

WebEx

Cisco's WebEx (www.webex.com) is perhaps the most-used web conferencing solution today. Various solutions and pricing plans are available, for organizations large and small. Features include VoIP support, integrated audio and video, application sharing, on-the-fly annotation, meeting recording and playback, and so on.

Figure 18.9 shows a typical WebEx presentation. In this example, a PowerPoint presentation is being annotated by the presenter, while participants are chatting in a pane on the right. The presenter, in this case, can also take notes during the course of the presentation; these notes appear in their own pane on the lower right.

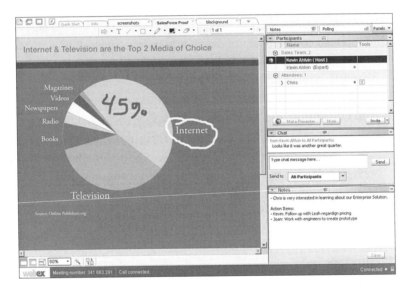

FIGURE 18.9

A WebEx presentation, complete with annotation and real-time text chat.

Yugma

Yugma (www.yugma.com) offers three different plans, priced from $199.95 to $899.85 per year based on how many people may attend a meeting. Features include desktop sharing, teleconferencing, public and private chat, annotations, and a whiteboard.

Zoho Meeting

Last but not least, Zoho Meeting (meeting.zoho.com) is, for now at least, a free web conferencing service. It includes the expected features, including application/desktop sharing, chat, and Skype integration, as well as remote PC control.

WHAT'S THE BEST WAY TO TALK?

There are multiple ways to communicate online because not every type of communication is the same. Nor, for that matter, do all users have the same communications preferences.

For our purposes, let's compare email with instant messaging. The reality is, you use instant messaging in different ways than you use email.

For example, instant messaging is ideal for very short, very immediate messages. (In fact, most instant messaging systems limit the length of the messages you can send through their systems.) On the other hand, email is better than instant messaging for communicating longer, more complex, and more formal messages.

If you want to compare each method of online communication with its offline equivalent, think of email as the online version of written letters and instant messaging as the online version of paging. You should use each application as appropriate for your own particular communication needs.

And what of web conferencing? This tool is the online equivalent of a group meeting. It's not a one-to-one communication (although one-on-one communications are still possible via private chat sessions), but rather a one-to-many presentation or many-to-many conversation. Think of web conferencing as a way to facilitate communications among all the members of your group—even if your group is spread out between a dozen or more locations.

Collaborating via Social Networks and Groupware

When it comes to collaborating with a group of people who may or may not share the same physical location, one naturally turns to the web. When all team members have access to the Internet, why not use the Internet to connect the members of the group—to enable communication, file sharing, and the like?

That's exactly what you can do, if you use the right tools. In this chapter, we discuss two such tools: social networks and online groupware. The former is a free but limited collaborate tool, while the latter has more functionality—but a typically higher price.

Creating Groups on Social Networks

You're probably already familiar with social networks such as Facebook and MySpace. The typical social network is a hosted site that aims to create a community of users, each of whom posts his or her own personal profile on the site. Each user includes enough person information in her profile to enable other users with similar interests to connect as "friends"; one's collection of friends helps to build a succession of personal communities.

Most profile pages include some form of blog, discussion forum, or chat space so that friends can communicate with the person profiled. In many instances, individual users also post a running list of their current activities so that their friends always know what they're up to.

Given that social networks are personal in nature, what value do they hold for businesses, community groups, and families? Lots, if you use them properly.

You see, most social networking sites let you create your own topic-specific groups. In this instance, a group is a collection of users who share the same interest; group members can communicate via discussion boards, share photos and videos, and even upload and download documents and other files.

In other words, a social network group is like a virtual meeting or community room. Instead of posting notices on a physical bulletin board, you post notices on a virtual message board. Instead of exchanging brochures and papers by hand, you upload photos, documents, and other files for all to share. And, because most social networks are free for all to use (in exchange for the occasional on-page advertisement), it's a cheap way to keep the members of your group up-to-date and organized.

In this regard, I find social network groups especially useful for community groups, far-flung friends, and families. You get just enough functionality to keep everyone in touch with each other, at no cost to anyone involved. No IT support is necessary, nor do you have to lease web hosting space; the social network site maintains all the servers and technology. And, of course, all of these sites are easy to join and easy to use, which is nice if your groups include non-tech-savvy members.

These social network groups are less useful for larger businesses. In a nutshell, these groups lack the advanced collaboration features that help to keep group projects on track. In addition, the profusion of web page advertising is anathema to many businesspeople. Finally, many businesses aren't comfortable posting their business on a nonsecure third-party site (nor should they be), especially when more secure options are available.

With all this in mind, let's take a quick look at the two most popular social networking sites (at least in the United States) and what they offer in terms of group collaboration features.

Facebook

Of all the social network sites, I recommend Facebook (www.facebook.com) first and foremost for those serious about group collaboration. Compared to MySpace, Facebook is more of a site for grown-ups; MySpace is more suited for teenagers and preteens.

When you create a group on Facebook, you end up with a group page like the one in Figure 19.1. A Facebook group includes the following collaborative features:

FIGURE 19.1

A Facebook group page.

- Recent news
- Discussion board
- Uploaded photos and videos
- Posted web pages
- The Wall—a kind of chat board

Your group can be Open (public), Closed (description if public, but members have to be approved), or Secret (membership by invitation only). Unfortunately, Facebook groups do not offer file uploading or sharing.

MySpace

A group on MySpace (www.myspace.com) is even more limited in functionality than what you can find on Facebook; this isn't surprising, given MySpace's typically younger audience. There's no file uploading, although members can upload group photos. There's a facility for posting group bulletins, and the obligatory discussion board, but that's it. Oh, and you have to put up with advertisements smack in the middle of your group page, as you can see in Figure 19.2. If you can live with all this, by all means consider MySpace for your (limited) group needs.

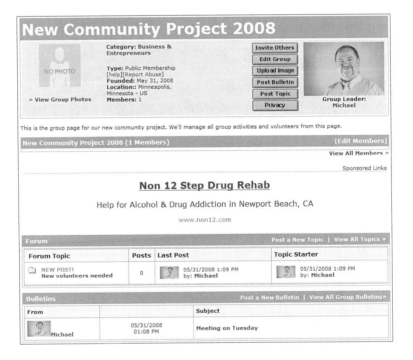

FIGURE 19.2

A MySpace group page.

Other Web Groups

The groups on social networking sites aren't the only groups you can create on the web. In fact, they may be some of the less-functional groups out there; other sites do groups better.

Case in point: Google Groups (groups.google.com). When you create a Google Group, you get the obligatory message forum, but you also get to upload and share files, as well as create topic-specific pages within the group; group members can be notified of new posts via email. A Google Group can be Public (anyone can join, but only members can read messages), Announcement-Only (anyone can join, but only moderators can post messages), or Restricted (only the people you invite can join).

Similar to Google Groups is Yahoo! Groups (groups.yahoo.com). Here you also get a message forum (with email notification of new posts) and file uploading, and also a photo library, group calendar, and polls. You can select whether your group appears in the Yahoo! Groups directory, whether anyone can join or if you have to approve all members, and who can post messages to the group.

Because of the file-uploading and -sharing options, either of these two groups might be more useful to you than a Facebook or MySpace group—even though they might not have the cachet of the social networking groups.

Evaluating Online Groupware

For larger businesses, a social network group probably won't suffice. What you need instead is a collection of web-based collaborative tools that help your team members not only communicate with each other but also manage their group projects.

This type of solution is commonly known as *groupware*, and when it's based in the cloud it's called *online groupware*. In a nutshell, groupware is collaboration software for workgroups. Online groupware does away with the physical constraints of traditional groupware, letting members from throughout an organization, in any location, access group assets.

What does this mean? In practicality, online groupware typically includes some or all of the following tools:

- File and document uploading and sharing
- Web calendar
- Task/project manager

- Message boards
- Text-based chat rooms / instant messaging
- Wiki-like collaborative pages
- Blogs

Why use online groupware? First of all, it puts all your group communications (and, in some cases, files) all in one place—and that one place is accessible to group members in any location, as long as they have an Internet connection. Second, groupware makes it easier to communicate, which should reduce the number of meetings and conferences calls, as well as your email traffic. Finally, all this should increase your group's collective and members' individual productivity. It's as simple as that.

For example, suppose you're managing a community not-for-profit group. You can use online groupware to connect other managers and volunteers across the community. You can share plans, proposals, and other documents with all members, and use the groupware to solicit and receive proposals and invoices from suppliers. And, best of all, you can do this from your own computer, which means fewer phone calls, car trips, and unnecessary meetings—all of which translates into less time involved and fewer expenses, both of which are important for charities.

So read on to learn about some of the most popular online groupware applications.

AirSet

AirSet (www.airset.com) provides a cloud-based website for your group. Your AirSet site can include group announcements, a web calendar, contact list, task list, instant messaging, wiki for collaborative publishing, blog, file sharing and online storage, photo albums, and music playlists. And with all these tools, when one person in the group makes a change, everyone else sees the updated information.

ContactOffice

ContactOffice (www.contactoffice.com) is a web-based data management system that lets you share emails, contacts, tasks, appointments, and documents with other group members. You can create internal or intercompany groups;

the latter helps you communicate with customers, suppliers, and other people outside your immediate office. You also get a web-based calendar, address book, message forum, and real-time chat. (Figure 19.3 shows the ContactOffice's "virtual office" dashboard page.)

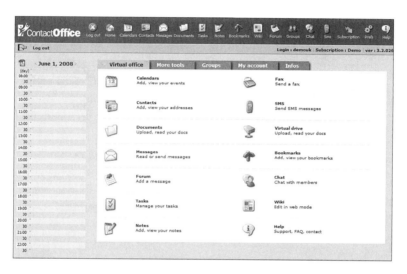

FIGURE 19.3

ContactOffice's "virtual office."

Google Sites

Google Sites (sites.google.com), formerly known as Jotspot, lets you create a group web page (hosted by Google), like the one shown in Figure 19.4. This page is completely customizable with your choice of file uploads, group announcements, task/project management, mailing lists, group calendar, and the like. Google Sites also integrates with Google's other online apps, including Gmail, Google Calendar, Google Docs, and Google Talk. And, as with most things Google, it's completely free.

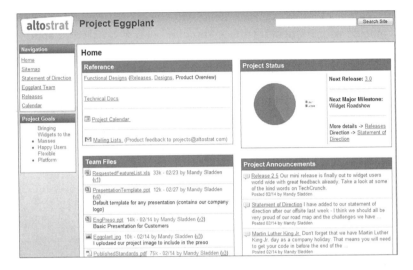

FIGURE 19.4
A typical Google Sites group page.

Huddle

Huddle (www.huddle.net) is a hosted environment that combines online collaboration, project management, and document sharing, using social networking principles. You create a network of collaborative team workspaces, managed from a central dashboard. You can then take advantage of Huddle's online file storage, project calendar, RSS and email notifications, whiteboard, wiki, and other collaborative tools.

Nexo

Nexo (www.nexo.com) lets you create a free personalized group website. The site can include photos, videos, forums, message boards, interactive calendars, polls, and to-do lists. Nexo targets its service to family, friend, and community groups, although it may also function for some less-demanding business groups. (Figure 19.5 shows a sample site for a youth sports team.)

note Nexo was recently acquired by Shutterfly.

FIGURE 19.5

A Nexo group site for a youth sports team.

OpenTeams

OpenTeams (www.openteams.com) is better suited for larger businesses. It offers team folders, blogging, and wiki-like collaborative pages, all monitored via a customizable Navigator page, shown in Figure 19.6. From here you can keep track of key team members, organize resources with tags, participate in threaded discussions, and monitor new content posted by team members. Pricing is on a per-user, per-use basis, starting at $0.99 per user log-on day.

FIGURE 19.6
The OpenTeams Navigator lets you monitor team members and content.

ProjectSpaces

ProjectSpaces (www.projectspaces.com) provides an online workspace designed especially for group collaboration. You get an online document library, email discussion lists, task management, group announcements via email and RSS, a shared group calendar, and shared group documents.

teamspace

Our final online groupware application is called teamspace (www.teamspace.com), with a lowercase *t*. This application offers task and project management, contact management, an online calendar, message forum, notice board, file sharing, text-based chat, and synchronization with Microsoft Outlook. Pricing is on a per-member basis, with additional fees for storage space used.

OLD-SCHOOL GROUPWARE

The concept of groupware, otherwise known as collaborative software, has been around for a long time, at least in terms of computer years. If you've ever used Lotus Notes or Microsoft Exchange, you've used groupware. These programs facilitate the sharing of calendars, the handling of email, and the replication of files across a local area network—typically within a single organization or even a single physical location.

Another pioneering groupware application was Groove, developed by Ray Ozzie, the same guy who developed Lotus Notes (and who has since gone on to the position of chief software architect at Microsoft). Ozzie started work on the Groove project in late 1997, after leaving Lotus; the first version of the application was released in 2000, and the program is still sold today, by Microsoft (its new owner).

Like the online groupware discussed in this chapter, Groove enables users to store and share contact information, send and receive text and voice messages, share files, and otherwise collaborate in real time. Far from being a cloud service, however, Groove is a peer-to-peer application. What that means is that all the tools and data for a group project are stored separately on each individual member's PC. The Groove software performs automatic background synchronization to ensure that each group member has the most recent version of each file.

Despite the local nature of Groove, it was the harbinger of today's cloud-based groupware solutions. It performs many of the same tasks and included many of the same tools; its only limitation is that it can be deployed only within a single enterprise, prohibiting the kind of global collaboration possible with newer cloud-based solutions.

Collaborating via Blogs and Wikis

G roup projects are all about collaboration and communication, so it pays to seek out every possible way to communicate with other group members. We've already looked at web mail and instant messaging, social network groups and groupware, but there are even more ways to handle your group communications.

The two communication methods we examine in this final chapter are both web based, even if they don't always fall neatly into the category of cloud computing. Blogs and wikis can both be housed in the cloud or on dedicated servers, depending on the service. But the point is that they're both web based and they both facilitate group collaboration. Read on to learn more.

Evaluating Blogs for Collaboration

If you've been on the Internet for any length of time, you've probably heard something about *blogs*. A blog (short for "web log") is a kind of online journal that its author updates frequently with new musings and information.

In terms of organization, a blog is a collection of individual *posts* or messages. The posts are arranged in reverse chronological order, with the newest posts at the top—which makes it easy to keep track of the latest developments. Older posts are relegated to the blog archives, which are generally accessible via a link in the sidebar column. And, at the end of each post, you'll find a link to comments; this is where blog readers can register their own personal comments about any given post.

> **note** Your blog posts don't have to be text only (although they can be). Most blogs let you include digital photos, blueprints, and other graphics, as well as audio and video files, in your posts.

But here's what makes blogs really powerful. A blog doesn't have to be the work of a single author; it can include posts from multiple contributors, as well as comments on each of those posts. This makes a blog ideal for keeping track of progress on a group project.

Here's how it goes. You create your blog, hosted on your company's servers or on a popular blogging tool such as Blogger or WordPad. You make it a private blog and assign authorship status to all the members of your team. This means that everyone on your team can initiate new posts, as well as comment on the posts of others.

When you have something important to say to the group, you make a blog post. Same with the other members; when they have updated info, they post it. In addition, other members can comment on your posts—for example, you can create a post to schedule a meeting, and have the other members comment on your post with their replies.

Members of your group can access the blog by navigating to its web page to see what's new, or subscribe to an RSS feed that will notify them whenever there's a new post to the blog, so they're never in the dark.

Where can your blog be hosted? If you work for a large company, ask your IT department about hosting your blog on the company's servers. Otherwise, you can check out any of the following blog-hosting communities, all of which will let you create private group blogs.

Blogger

Blogger (www.blogger.com) is Google's blog-hosting community, and with more than 8 million individual blogs, the largest blog host on the Internet. All Blogger blogs are free, which contributes to their popularity.

The Blogger Dashboard, shown in Figure 20.1, is where you manage all your blog activity. From here you can create new blog posts, edit comments to your posts, manage your Blogger account and profile, and access Blogger's help system. It's also where you create a new blog.

FIGURE 20.1

Managing your blog via the Blogger Dashboard.

Creating a new Blogger blog is as easy as filling in a few forms. After you click the Create a Blog link in the Blogger Dashboard, you're asked to enter a title for your blog and a corresponding blog address (the part of the URL that goes before Blogger's blogspot.com domain). Next, you get to choose a template for your blog—a predesigned combination of page layout, colors, and fonts. Blogger now creates your blog—and you're ready to start posting.

Figure 20.2 shows a typical Blogger blog— if there is such a beast as a "typical" blog. You can customize your blog with any number of different templates and color schemes; you can also add a variety of gadgets and other nonpost page elements.

note By default, Blogger serves as host for your blog, and assigns you a URL in the blogspot.com domain. If you'd rather host your blog on your own website, that option is also available.

FIGURE 20.2

A "typical" Blogger blog—for the author's book Googlepedia: The Ultimate Google Resource.

Of course, one of the things you'll want to customize is the list of people who have access to you blog. By default, a Blogger blog is completely public, and anyone on the Internet can read it. However, there's a way to make your blog private so that only invited guests can view it; just go to the Blogger Dashboard, click the Manage: Settings link, and then click the Permissions link. When the next page appears, go to the Blog Readers section and select who can view your blog: Anybody (keeps the blog public), Only People I Choose, or Only Blog Authors.

For a group blog, the option you want is Only Blog Authors. Of course, you now have to invite the other members of your group to be blog authors; do this by clicking the Add Authors button.

note In Blogger parlance, a *blog author* is someone who, like you, can create new blog postings. Although anyone can add comments to existing postings, only blog authors can create new postings.

TypePad

TypePad (www.typepad.com) is quite similar to Blogger. You can customize your
blog with a number of different designs
and widgets, and you can select multiple
coauthors for your blog. However, TypePad
isn't free; you pay anywhere from $4.95 to

note Facebook, MySpace, and other social networks also include blogs as part of their profile pages—as do many online groupware and web-based desktop applications.

$89.95 per month, depending on the features you want. (You need at least the
Pro plan, starting at $14.95/month, to support multiple co-authors.)

WordPress

WordPress (www.wordpress.com) is another popular blog-hosting community.
It's a lot like both Blogger and TypePad, but perhaps a bit more customizable.
You get lots of themes to choose from, sidebar widgets, and a private mem-
bers-only option. You also can create multiple blogs and assign multiple
authors. And, like Blogger, a WordPress blog is completely free.

Evaluating Wikis for Collaboration

Our final method of group collaboration is the wiki. You're probably familiar
with the concept of wikis, thanks to the web's most popular wiki—Wikipedia.

If you've never used Wikipedia (www.wikipedia.org), you're in for an eye
opener. Wikipedia is, in essence, a giant online encyclopedia—but with a
twist. Wikipedia's content is created solely by the site's users, resulting in the
world's largest online collaboration. Wikipedia articles are written, edited, and
elaborated on by people of all types, from students, to subject-matter experts
and professional researchers, to interested amateurs. It's a true group collaboration.

Which is, in fact, what a wiki is—a collection of web pages where any users
can contribute or modify content. The first
wiki was WikiWikiWeb, a website founded
in 1995 to facilitate the exchange of ideas
between computer programmers. Wikis
enable all users not only to write new articles, but also to comment on and edit
existing articles.

note The word *wiki* comes from the Hawaiian word for "fast"—and is not an acronym for "what I know is," as some suggest.

Today, many organizations use wikis as collaborative applications. A group wiki can be public (open to all users), as Wikipedia is, or private—which is ideal for project groups, businesses, and other organizations.

A private wiki invites all group members to create new pages on the wiki site or to edit any existing page. All writing and editing is done within the web browser, no extra software or tools necessary. In most instances, there is no review of the articles or edits before they're accepted.

The result is a collection of articles or documents, written collaboratively. The wiki software organizes the articles behind the scenes and manages the versioning for each article.

Do you think a wiki is a good tool for your particular organization or project? If so, check out the following wiki hosting services; they make it easy to get your wiki up and running and to manage it on an ongoing basis.

PBwiki

PBwiki (www.pbwiki.com) offers various levels of wiki hosting. Small wikis (one to three users) are free; larger ones are priced as low as $4 per user per month. Wiki creation is easy, thanks to a variety of premade templates. You also get online file storage to help you organize your other documents as part of your wiki.

Versionate

Versionate (www.versionate.com) offers hosted wikis designed for group collaboration. A Versionate wiki is business friendly, thanks to SSL-level security and full control over editing privileges; you can also import Word, Excel, PowerPoint, and PDF documents into your wiki. The company offers several different plans: Free (500MB storage), Personal (2GB storage for $2/month), Business (unlimited storage for $25/month), and Enterprise (unlimited storage for $2/user/month).

wikihost.org

The wikihost.org site (www.wikihost.org) provides free wiki hosting. Wiki creation is via the GeboBebo engine, which offers a local database structure, user and rights management, RSS feeds and email notification for new and updated articles, and image and file uploading.

Wikispaces

Wikispaces (www.wikispaces.com) claims to host more than 450,000 individual wikis. Standard features include image and file uploading, widget and media embedding, RSS feeds and email notifications, discussion areas, and detailed user statistics. A variety of hosting plans are available, from Basic (free) to Private Label Premium ($800/month).

Zoho Wiki

Finally, from our friends at Zoho, comes their wiki application, Zoho Wiki (wiki.zoho.com). They offer free wiki hosting complete with WYSIWYG editing, versioning of wiki pages, and the ability to make your wiki public or private—all for free. Your wiki is managed from a Dashboard page, like the one shown in Figure 20.3; just click the New Page icon to add a new page to the wiki.

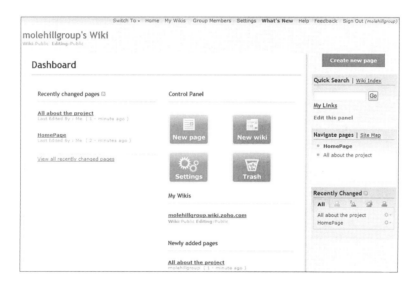

FIGURE 20.3
Using the Zoho Wiki Dashboard to manage a wiki.

IS CLOUD COMPUTING NECESSARY FOR GROUP COLLABORATION?

This is book is all about cloud computing, yet many of the collaboration and communication tools discussed in this section aren't technically cloud services. That is, many of these tools either exist solely on a dedicated server (such as a company's internal server) or work via peer-to-peer technology. Knowing this, just how necessary is cloud computing for effective group collaboration?

The answer, of course, is not totally necessary. After all, you can easily use noncloud tools, such as instant messaging, to communicate with other members of your group. And, if your group is 100 percent internal to your company, there's no reason to venture into the cloud at all—assuming you always have access to your company's network, of course.

But if you want to include people from outside your organization in your group, or if your group is spread out between multiple locations, or if members of your group travel or work from home, then incorporating some cloud-based tools makes a lot of sense. When you're out of the main office, it's a lot easier to log on to a cloud website than it is to try to remotely tunnel into your company's network.

That's not to say that pure cloud technology is always necessary. Your application and documents could just as easily be hosted on the hosting provider's servers; they don't have to be "in the cloud," per se. That said, as applications become bigger and more powerful, and as the need for huge amounts of storage continues to increase, the advantages of sharing cloud resources become more explicit.

So even if your groupware and collaboration applications aren't yet hosted in the cloud, they probably will be sometime in the future. It's simply a lot more efficient to share space on hundreds or thousands of cloud computers than it is to keep buying more servers for your data center. That's the real reason why cloud computing will likely become ubiquitous; it provides more power and storage for less money than any other current computing solution.

Index

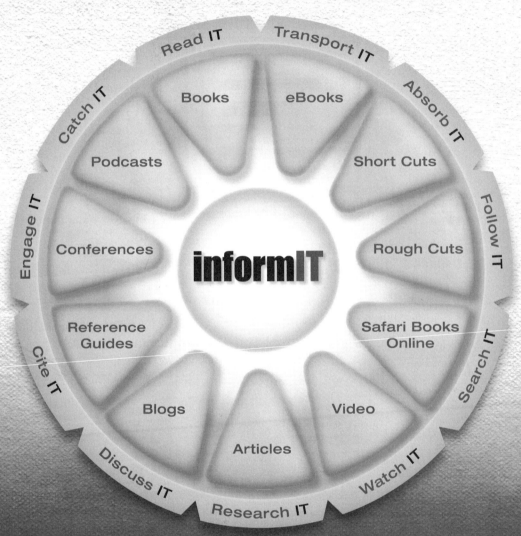

LearnIT at InformIT

Go Beyond the Book

Read IT · Transport IT · Absorb IT · Follow IT · Search IT · Watch IT · Research IT · Discuss IT · Cite IT · Engage IT · Catch IT

Books · eBooks · Short Cuts · Rough Cuts · Safari Books Online · Video · Articles · Blogs · Reference Guides · Conferences · Podcasts

informIT

11 WAYS TO LEARN IT at **www.informIT.com/learn**

The digital network for the publishing imprints of Pearson Education

FREE Online Edition

Your purchase of **Cloud Computing** includes access to a free online edition for 45 days through the Safari Books Online subscription service. Nearly every Que book is available online through Safari Books Online, along with over 5,000 other technical books and videos from publishers such as Addison-Wesley Professional, Cisco Press, Exam Cram, IBM Press, O'Reilly, Prentice Hall, and Sams.

SAFARI BOOKS ONLINE allows you to search for a specific answer, cut and paste code, download chapters, and stay current with emerging technologies.

Activate your FREE Online Edition at
www.informit.com/safarifree

> **STEP 1:** Enter the coupon code: 8DEV-FNIG-USBN-HXFT-5DA6.

> **STEP 2:** New Safari users, complete the brief registration form. Safari subscribers, just login.

If you have difficulty registering on Safari or accessing the online edition, please e-mail customer-service@safaribooksonline.com